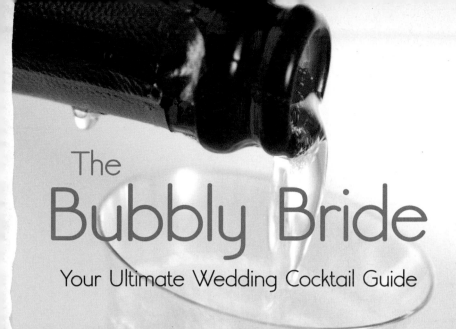

The
Bubbly Bride
Your Ultimate Wedding Cocktail Guide

Natalie Bovis-Nelsen
The Liquid Muse

Photographs by Claire Barrett

gpp®
life

Guilford, Connecticut
An imprint of Globe Pequot Press

GPP Life is an imprint of Globe Pequot Press.

The Liquid Muse Sustainable Sips is a registered trademark of Natalie
Bovis-Nelsen.

Design by Diana Nuhn

Photo on p. 73 by Susan Bourgoin © Morris Book Publishing, LLC
All other photographs by Claire Barrett © Morris Book Publishing, LLC

Library of Congress Cataloging-in-Publication Data
Bovis-Nelsen, Natalie.
  The bubbly bride : your ultimate wedding cocktail guide / Natalie Bovis-
Nelsen ; photographs by Claire Barrett.
     p. cm.
  ISBN 978-1-59921-467-2
  1. Cocktails. 2. Weddings—Planning. I. Title.
  TX951.B766 2009
  647.95747—dc22

                                                    2009022536

Printed in China

10 9 8 7 6 5 4 3 2 1

*This book is dedicated to
my wonderful husband, Jason,
with a special nod to our families
and friends who clink glasses with us
throughout life's celebrations.*

Cheers &

Natalie Bovis Nelson

Contents

Here Comes the Bride!

CONGRATULATIONS! You met the guy, you got the ring, you said, "Yes, I'll marry you." Now begins the intoxicating journey toward THE BIG DAY! Along the way you'll have many celebrations, a few trials and tribulations, and a lot of decisions to make.

Containing your excitement—and your stress—can take a lot out of you. Of course, it's easy to get crabby when the rest of the world doesn't grind to a screeching halt just because *you* are getting married. (Doesn't everyone realize what a big darn deal this is?!) Luckily the Bride-to-Be gets lots of "free passes" to stamp her feet and insist on having everything done her way. The bride is the star of the show, after all.

Still, in the long run, it behooves you to waft gracefully through wedding planning with a healthy dose of diplomacy—and, perhaps, a little nip of liquid tranquility from time to time. Do yourself (and everyone else) the favor of taking a moment to relax once in a while amid the hullabaloo. Get a massage, go for a walk, and whip up a batch of special drinkies for the friends and family who rally around you. Learning to negotiate stressful events with style and charm will serve you well throughout the wedding planning—and the marriage!

On the following pages, you will learn everything you need to know from the moment you've sealed the deal with a kiss. In some cases planning a wedding means a year's worth of gatherings leading up to the *grand finale.* An engagement party gives you a chance to make the big announcement with panache. Then come bridal showers, luncheons, and the "watch out world, I'm getting hitched" bachelorette party (all while watching your figure for the catwalk down the aisle). Finally, the Wedding Day arrives and you get to revel in the spotlight as guests bless your union and give sappy speeches.

But, don't think it's over yet! Many couples host a brunch

the day after the wedding, particularly if many guests had to travel from far away; of course, as soon as you're back from the honeymoon, you'll be dying to try out all the gorgeous stemware you received from your gift registry. Eventually, you will get to spend eternity in wedded bliss *à deux,* but there's a lot of entertaining to do first, and nearly all of it includes cocktails. Luckily, this little guide has fallen into your hands to help you navigate the months ahead, ensuring that you—and your loved ones—will raise the perfect drink at every toasting opportunity.

I custom design cocktails for all sorts of high-end events, including weddings. So I've written a whole chapter on how to create your own signature cocktail employing the philosophies and techniques of quality mixology: freshly squeezed juices, a dash of bitters, muddled herbs. I've also included some classic cocktail recipes to use as a guide. This is one aspect of wedding planning your fiancé won't mind: designing a love-inspired libation that you can not only share with your guests, but also enjoy for years to come.

Although this book is chock full of my own creations, I thought it would be fun to invite some of my bartender friends from around the United States to contribute their original recipes as well. A wedding is about bringing loved ones together, isn't it? Your fiancé will especially appreciate the Boys' Night Out section, which is dedicated to the bachelor party and features recipes created by guys for guys. His celebration should be punctuated with quality drinks, too!

Whether planning an intimate ceremony for close friends and family or an outrageous affair for hundreds of guests—or even if you plan to scrap it all at the last minute and elope—these cocktails will take you from "I will" to "I do!" and ensure that you drink happily ever after.

Part 1

Building Your Love Nest:
The Liquid Muse Home Bar Basics

One fun part of wedding planning for both you and your groom is picking out items for your gift registry. In addition to china, linens, and newfangled kitchen appliances, any cocktail lover needs to register for some specific glassware to make the home bar complete. Keep in mind that these are things you will use often and can break, so you might want to choose common styles that can be easily replaced or interchanged.

Along with glasses, you will need a few essential bar tools to make the drinks properly. I suggest a few cocktail books in the event that you catch cocktail party fever, and I've also listed some ingredients to keep on hand so you are prepared to make your favorite drinks anytime. Some of these items may not be available on gift registries . . . but won't it be fun adding them to your bar collection over the years to come?

The Tools of the Trade

BAR SPOON: A spoon with a very long stem. It works especially well for reaching the bottom of a mixing glass or other tall glasses.

CITRUS PRESS: A one-step tool for squeezing the juice from a lemon or lime half. The larger ones can accommodate half an orange or small grapefruit. (The press doubles as a convenient kitchen tool—I highly recommend having at least one!)

COCKTAIL SHAKER: I recommend a Boston shaker, which comes in two parts: the mixing glass and the tin lid. I like this one because you can see the ingredients as you make the drink. When you secure the tin lid on top of the glass, the shaker will seal and remain secure. Give it a good whack on the side to unseal it when you're ready to pour out the drink. If you prefer a three-part shaker (which has the strainer built in), there are many fun styles—why not start your own collection?

ENTERTAINING ITEMS: Don't forget a few cool accessories. Serving trays, a nice ice bucket and ice scoop, and wine and cognac decanters make your home bar look like a class act.

ICE TRAYS: Good drinks start with quality ice. Don't rely on your automatic freezer's ice cubes or a bag of ice from the corner store. Big, solid ice cubes cool the drink more effectively during shaking and melt more slowly in the glass. Also, experiment with freezing tonic water or fruit juices, so your drink gets replenished as the cubes melt. Freezing raspberries or blueberries with the liquid in the ice cube trays makes for

decorative and tasty additions to your cocktails! Use purified water for the best-tasting drinks.

JIGGER: A two-sided tool used for measuring liquid ingredients. The larger side typically measures a "jigger," or 1½ ounces, and the smaller side measures a "pony," or 1 ounce. It is a good idea to own other combinations with ¾- or ½-ounce measures as well.

JULEP STRAINER: This perforated, spoon-shaped strainer fits snuggly into the mixing glass to hold back ice, if you stir a drink rather than shake it in the tin (as you would with a classic Martini or Manhattan).

MUDDLER: This is basically a pestle (as used in cooking) with a longer handle so it can reach the bottom of a mixing glass.

WIRE STRAINER: If you buy a Boston shaker, it will not have a built-in strainer, so choose one that fits well over the opening of the mixing glass. It is best to strain the liquid over fresh ice cubes in a glass rather than serve the drink with the partially melted ones in the shaker.

How to rim a glass: Rub the rim of a cocktail glass with a piece of lemon or lime, while holding the glass upside down. Dip the rim onto a small plate of granulated sugar, or into a tin of rimming sugar. Set aside while you prepare the drink.

Stemware

Everything tastes better when sipped from sexy stemware
(and you look better drinking it, too!). If you don't already have
elegant glassware, your wedding registry is time to indulge.
Your love nest is not complete without proper glasses! This list
of glassware corresponds to the simplistic way I've described
the glasses for the drinks in this book (they may vary slightly
if you have a bar manual or individual department store).
I suggest registering for at least 8 pieces of any kinds of
glassware you choose.

BAR MUG: A thick, heat-resistant glass mug used for beer
or hot drinks

CHAMPAGNE COUPE/SAUCER: A round, saucer-shaped
champagne glass

CHAMPAGNE FLUTE: A tall, narrow glass designed especially
for sparkling wine

COCKTAIL GLASS: Any glass used for a cocktail which is
not otherwise defined in this list. (My personal collection
of vintage cocktail glasses is featured in the photos in this
book.)

MARGARITA GLASS: A very wide-rimmed, bowl-shaped glass
used especially for margaritas

MARTINI GLASS: A V-shaped glass (traditionally 6 ounces)
with a tall, thin stem

 **ROCKS GLASS:** A short, stout glass intended for drinks served "on the rocks" (over ice)

SHOT GLASS: A small glass that typically holds about 1 ounce of liquid

TALL GLASS: A large tumbler used for mixed drinks; often called a Collins glass or highball glass

WINE GLASS: A smaller, narrower glass used for white wine

WINE GOBLET: A wider, rounder wine glass used for red wine. The wider bowl allows for swirling and more air contact with the wine, which allows a good red to "open" or "breathe" in the glass.

From the Kitchen

Some basic cooking tools are useful in your home bar, as well.

BLENDER: For smoothie-style drinks

CUTTING BOARD: For preparing garnishes, cutting fruit

FOOD PROCESSOR: Makes crushing ice, grinding dry goods, and pureeing fruits and vegetables quick and easy

JUICER: Freshly juiced fruits and vegetables, rather than frozen or bottled, make all the difference in the quality of your cocktails

PARING KNIFE: This should be small and sharp for cutting fruit and vegetables

PEELER: Helpful to easily remove the skin from cucumbers, pears, apples, etc.

Liquid Assets: Stocking the Bar

Creating a home together includes investing in your first shared "liquid assets," i.e., stocking your home bar!

ACCESSORIES: Maraschino cherries, drink umbrellas, swizzle sticks, cocktail picks, coasters, flavored rimming sugar (Stirrings and Cocktail Candy are two companies that make the latter.)

BITTERS: Keep a bottle each of Angostura and Peychaud's on hand, and don't forget to experiment with flavored bitters, too!

DAIRY: Milk, whipping cream, or half-and-half

EXOTIC INGREDIENTS: Coconut milk, açaí juice, lychees, edible flowers, Thai chilis, jalapeños, rose water, yuzu juice

FRESH FRUIT AND/OR FRUIT JUICES (buy fresh as needed, use frozen when out of season): Lemons, limes, blood oranges, grapefruit, pineapple, watermelon, cantaloupe, honeydew, mangoes, peaches, apricots, raspberries, blueberries, blackberries, cherries, strawberries, pomegranates, guava

FRESH HERBS (buy as needed): Basil, dill, rosemary, cilantro, thyme, mint

FRUIT PUREES: Buy frozen fruit purees in a store or make your own with this basic recipe: Blend ½ cup fresh or frozen fruit with ½ cup sugar and ½ ounce lemon juice.

FRESH VEGETABLES: Tomatoes, cucumbers, celery

MIXERS: Club soda, ginger ale, tonic water, flavored waters, flavored Italian spritzers, flavored diet sodas (for low-cal cocktails)

SPICES AND CONDIMENTS: Fresh ginger, black pepper, cayenne pepper, Worcestershire sauce, horseradish, agave honey, Tabasco, sugar, cloves, cinnamon sticks, wasabi

Plant a "cocktail garden" in your yard or on your balcony. Even a windowsill can be home to a variety of herbs, hot peppers, and vegetables integral to muddling fresh cocktails!

SIMPLE SYRUP

Simple syrup is essentially sugar-water cooked into a syrup. It is easy to use for sweetening cocktails because the sugar is already dissolved and won't leave granules in the drink.

2 cups granulated white sugar
1 cup water

Pour sugar and water into a small saucepan and, stirring constantly, bring mixture to a boil. Reduce heat to low and let simmer for 3-5 minutes, stirring occasionally. Cool and refrigerate in a glass jar or plastic bottle.

For a thinner syrup, use a 1:1 ratio of sugar and water.

SIMPLE SYRUP VARIATIONS:

Raw sugar simple syrup: For some drinks (especially organic cocktails or those with rum, cachaça, or whisky) I like to use raw brown sugar. It has a slightly more distinctive flavor and can be a slightly healthier option than granulated white sugar.

Ginger-infused simple syrup: Add a 1-inch piece of peeled ginger to the saucepan, and follow simple syrup directions.

Lavender-infused simple syrup: Add ¼ cup dried lavender buds to the saucepan, and follow simple syrup directions.

Rose-Infused simple syrup: Follow simple syrup directions, but substitute rose water for plain water. (Potable rose water can be found in specialty stores and Middle Eastern markets.)

Tea-infused simple syrup: Follow simple syrup directions, but substitute tea for plain water.

Wildflower honey syrup: Follow simple syrup directions, but substitute honey for sugar.

Herb-infused simple syrup (thyme, rosemary): Follow simple syrup directions, but add a few leaves plucked from the stem of the herb plant.

Homemade sweet-n-sour: Blend equal parts simple syrup and fresh lemon juice. You won't want the premade, store-bought sweet-n-sour after you taste the difference that using fresh ingredients makes!

Part 2

Create Your Own Signature Cocktail

High-end events around the world are punctuated with a customized signature cocktail, so why should your wedding be any different? Following the guidelines in this chapter, you and your fiancé can make wedding planning *fun* by designing your own drink. Consider coming up with a name for the drink to reflect something about you as a couple, maybe a special place you visited together or something to do with the theme of your wedding.

Begin building your signature cocktail by choosing a kind of alcohol you both love. Maybe you want to use spirits or ingredients that are reflective of your cultures or heritage, as in Puerto Rican rum, French champagne, Brazilian cachaça, English or Dutch gin, or Japanese sake. Garnishes are also a creative way to tie in colors or other elements highlighted in your celebration.

Print your signature cocktail recipe on coasters to put on the bar at your wedding reception!

You have leeway to make anything that tastes great to you, of course, but putting substance before style will ensure a good outcome. In other words, don't choose a lesser-quality liquor for its color alone. Pink, purple, blue, or green liquid might look interesting in the bottle, but if the cocktail tastes like artificial ingredients, you and your guests will be sold short.

This chapter lays out a few basic mixology rules and gives an overview of spirits, incorporating examples of classic cocktails throughout.

Crash Course in Cocktails

Before we get into mixing and matching, shaking and stirring, I'd like to give you an overview of cocktails: where they come from and what goes into them. This quick introduction to basic mixology will help you design the perfect drink for your dream wedding. It will also set you up to make fabulous cocktails with all the cool barware you'll get as wedding gifts!

WHAT IS A COCKTAIL?

Today, the word cocktail gets used as a blanket term for all alcoholic beverages served in a glass. Originally, though, a cocktail was one classification of many kinds of mixed drinks. The word first appeared in print in 1803 in the United States, where the cocktail was invented. The definition of a true cocktail is: spirit + water + sugar + bitters. Let's break that down:

SPIRIT—any kind of distilled alcohol, including vodka, gin, tequilla, rum, whiskey, cognac, and so on

WATER—can be in the form of ice or soda water, for example

SUGAR—a sweetener, such as granulated sugar, simple syrup, honey, agave nectar, or sweet cordials

BITTERS—bark, herbs, and/or roots that have been brewed in alcohol. Heralded for their medicinal qualities, bitters have been used to settle minor gastric ailments for more than two centuries. A few drops added to a cocktail work as a flavor booster. Created in 1824 by a German physicist living in Venezuela, Angostura bitters are carried in most

supermarkets. Peychaud's bitters were developed by an apothecary named Antoine Amadee Peychaud in the early 1800s, in New Orleans, and used for drinks such as the Sazerac. Today, a range of flavored bitters such as orange, peach, grapefruit, rhubarb, whiskey barrel, etc., can be found in specialty stores.

LESS IS MORE!

Too many cocktail menus today feature swimming-pool-size "martini" drinks. It is crazy to think that anyone needs 10- or 12-ounce glasses filled with cheap booze and neon-colored sugary mixers. They are full of artificial ingredients and loaded with sugar—which will ensure a hangover. Not to mention, by the time you've worked halfway through a megasize cocktail, it has probably reached room temperature, so it doesn't taste as good.

When cocktails were created, the recipes were made to nestle nicely into 4- or 5-ounce stemware. The glasses were handcrafted and sometimes engraved or rimmed with silver or gold. They were delicate works of art, and the cocktails that went into them were treated as such.

The classic cocktails featured in this book typically measure less than 6 ounces. Keep that in mind when creating your signature cocktail and when registering for your glassware.

A Sip of Cocktail History:

Although Prohibition nearly killed the thriving American cocktail culture in the early 20th century, it opened the way for respectable women to sip alcoholic drinks alongside men. It had previously been considered unseemly for ladies to socialize in bars, but it was perfectly acceptable for them to enjoy teahouses or coffee shops. From 1920 to 1933, while Prohibition was in effect, "speakeasies" (secret saloons) could be entered only via a hidden door or password. These bars were often disguised as "soft drink" parlors, so who could blame a woman for being there? Obviously, we never left!

Get to Know Your Spirits and Classic Cocktails

Sometimes when I mention tequila, gin, or whiskey in one of my cocktail classes, I'm met with grimaces and groans from the female attendees. By and large, women aren't encouraged to appreciate a fine scotch or punctuate a special occasion with an aged cognac. While boys are initiated into the world of spirits with a glass of something dad is drinking, a slap on the back, and an "atta boy," we gals are lectured on the dangers of drinking alcohol.

This means that many of our earliest experiences with alcohol sprang from youthful rebellion or curiosity, when we tried things like tequila "poppers," or "jungle juice" in big plastic cups at college parties. Before what I jokingly call the Cosmo Revolution, women didn't belly up to the bar in droves to order martinis. And when entertaining at home, we were rarely encouraged to think beyond wine.

Luckily all that has changed. Today, women buy more wine than men, and they are branching out into the world of spirits. Articles about cocktails and mixologists are popping up in women's magazines, and drink recipes regularly appear on television shows and popular food-focused Web sites.

As adults, we can learn to appreciate a fine drink the way we do our favorite foods: as something to look forward to, savor, and enjoy with friends on a regular basis. Foodies know which rice makes the perfect risotto, which cut of beef results in a tender steak. Likewise, the cocktail enthusiast ought to know a bit about where each spirit comes from and how it is made. This base knowledge will help you successfully mix spirits and other ingredients into a delicious cocktail.

I try to educate myself continually with regard to wine, spirits, and cocktails. Some of the information below is highlighted in the Beverage Alcohol Resource (BAR) course, which I completed in 2008. It is the modern spirits professional's certification program, so I trust the information provided in the course, and the recipes presented, to be authentic.

VODKA

The current accepted definition for vodka is "a tasteless, odorless neutral spirit," and it can be made from just about anything. By fermenting and distilling grain, potatoes, grapes, even sugar beets, you can make vodka. The original ingredient directly impacts how the final spirit tastes. For example, wheat-based vodka is a little creamier than rye-based vodka, which tends to be a little spicier.

In relation to other spirits, vodka's characteristics don't stand out immediately, which makes it a good base or substitute spirit for all sorts of cocktails. But keep your mind open to experimenting with other spirits. After all, beige is not the only color in your box of crayons!

Vodka didn't become popular in the United States until after World War II. Its popularity spread in the 1950s, and around 1967 it surpassed gin, the original spirit used in martinis! By 1976 vodka was the most widely sold alcohol in the United States, and today it makes up more than 30% of liquor sales worldwide.

GIN

In the most simplistic terms, we can describe gin as juniper-infused grain vodka. A good gin can have herbaceous notes with a bit of zippy citrus, and sometimes slight floral qualities. It is the founding spirit of many classic cocktails ranging from Aviations to gimlets to martinis.

Some think that gin came from England, but English soldiers first learned about gin from the Dutch about 500 years ago. Once embraced by the British, gin traveled to all corners of the globe, including India, where the gin and tonic became a popular drink and medicinal remedy. Sailors drank quinine in tonic to stave off malaria, and the lime garnish helped keep scurvy at bay. What better excuse for a refreshing drink?

"Bathtub gin" refers to the clear spirit made during Prohibition. Jugs of it were often poured into a bathing tub so it could be mixed with water to dilute the alcohol proof and make the rough, foul-tasting rotgut slightly easier to swallow.

▼ AVIATION COCKTAIL
(Cocktail Glass)

This is a charming little gin drink created around 1910. A few drops of floral and fragrant Crème de Violette give it a sky blue color.

2 ounces gin
½ ounce maraschino liqueur
½ ounce lemon juice
Dash crème de violette

Shake all ingredients with ice. Strain into a vintage cocktail glass.

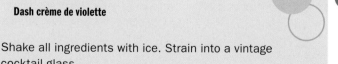

TEQUILA

Like Champagne in France, Tequila is a region in Mexico. The spirit is made from mashed, cooked, and fermented juices from the blue agave plant, which is a succulent and a member of the lily family. (It is not a cactus, like many people mistakenly assume.) Agave plants grow in the Mexican desert and look something like a big aloe plant, only they have hard oval centers called the piña (because it looks similar to an oversize pineapple). The plants aren't harvested until they are six, eight, or even ten years old.

The resulting tequila can be aged in wood barrels to give it a richer color and taste. Tequila's age is reflected in its categorization. *Blanco* is barely aged, if at all. *Reposado* is "rested," or aged for a few months. *Añejo* is aged for about a year. *Extra Añejo* is aged longer than a year or two. Tequila actually falls into the Mescal category, although in the United States we differentiate "tequila" from "mescal" by the distinctive treatment of the piña: For what we refer to as "mescal," the piña is roasted over flames rather than cooked in an oven, giving the resulting liquid a smoky flavor.

Once I learned to appreciate a fine añejo in a brandy snifter—no differently than I would an esteemed cognac—my whole perception of tequila changed. I loathe putting anything beyond a squeeze of lime in a fine, old tequila or mescal purely because the spirit is so layered and rich in flavor on its own. However, a good cocktail begins with good ingredients. Begin with good tequila, add fresh lime juice, homemade simple syrup or agave nectar, and a splash of orange liqueur, and you've got a killer margarita . . . with absolutely no sweet-n-sour or margarita mix!

CLASSIC MARGARITA

(Margarita Glass or Cocktail Glass)

The Spanish word *margarita* means "daisy." This drink, created in the 1930s, was originally called the Tequila Daisy.

2 ounces tequila

1 ounce orange liqueur

¾ ounce lime Juice

½ ounce simple syrup (optional, page 9)

Shake all ingredients and gently strain into a salt-rimmed glass.

RUM

Most rum comes from the Caribbean region and is made from molasses. However, Brazilian rum, made from fermented and distilled sugarcane juice, is called cachaça and its hallmark cocktail, the caipirinha, is growing in popularity worldwide. Rum gets its color from aging in wood, although sometimes caramel color is added to make the rum look as if it has been aged. Rum was so important during the British colonial era that each sailor was given a rum ration as part of his pay!

WHISKEY

Whiskey is a broad category encompassing Scotch whisky, Irish whiskey, Canadian whiskey, and American whiskeys such as bourbon, Tennessee whiskey, and rye. There is even a growing interest in Japanese whiskey! In the interest of keeping this brief, here's a very general overview.

Scotch whisky begins its differentiation with its spelling (no e). It is made from malted barley and/or grains. Irish whiskey is made from corn or barley. Canadian whiskey is mostly made from rye or corn, and it legally can be blended with sherry or fruit wines for extra flavor. Bourbon is made primarily in Kentucky and must be at least 51% corn. Tennessee whiskey is also at least 51% corn and comes from—you guessed it—Tennessee. Japanese whiskey is primarily made from malted barley, like Scotch. (At one time, the Japanese even went so far as to import Scottish water for blending!) All whiskeys are typically aged in oak barrels, which give them their color and enhance their taste.

MANHATTAN COCKTAIL
(Martini Glass)

Many women shy away from whiskey, but I encourage everyone to try a properly made classic Manhattan at least once. You may just find your new favorite drink!

2 ounces whiskey (rye or bourbon, depending on your preference)
1 ounce sweet vermouth
Dash Angostura bitters

Pour all ingredients into an ice-filled mixing glass. Rather than shake this drink, stir it with a bar spoon for at least 30 seconds. (Incidentally, a classic martini is stirred, too!) Strain it into a martini glass and garnish with a cherry or twist of lemon.

BRANDY

Brandy is made by distilling fermented fruit juice—primarily fermented grape juice—so it's little wonder that cognac, some of the best brandy, comes from the Champagne region of France. Other kinds of brandy include Armagnac (also French), Brandy de Jerez from Spain, and Pisco from South America.

Pisco has an interesting history. When the Spanish sailed to the areas known today as Peru and Chile, they brought grape vines to make wine for Mass. The grapes flourished, and the settlers began to distill the extra fermented grape juice into brandy. Today, both Chile and Peru claim Pisco as a proprietary spirit, and each considers the Pisco Sour its national drink.

 PISCO SOUR
(Cocktail Glass)

One taste of this delicious cocktail, and you will understand why two countries continue a friendly battle of "sour grapes" over claiming rights to it!

1½ ounces pisco

1 ounce simple syrup, page 9

¾ ounce freshly squeezed lemon juice

1 egg white

Dash Angostura bitters

Pour first four ingredients into a mixing glass. Dry shake for a few seconds. Fill with ice and shake vigorously for at least 30 seconds to make the egg white frothy. Strain into a small cocktail glass. Sprinkle a few drops of bitters on the foam.

A WORD ABOUT ABSINTHE

After being outlawed for most of the 20th century, absinthe is once again legal in the United States! There is a lot of misinformation surrounding absinthe. It has been rumored to make people go mad; it supposedly made Vincent van Gogh cut off his own ear, for example. There are stories of people hallucinating when they drink it, and among the writers, artists,

▼ THE SAZERAC
(Cocktail Glass)

Thanks to the unrelenting efforts of Ann Rogers Tuennerman, who is the founder of Tales of the Cocktail, an important annual cocktail conference held in New Orleans each summer, this classic drink—created in the Big Easy—became the city's official cocktail in 2008.

1 teaspoon absinthe
1 sugar cube
Dash Peychaud bitters
2 ounces rye whiskey

Swirl absinthe around a cocktail glass. Once coated, pour out the remaining liquid. Place the sugar cube in the glass, soak it with bitters. Muddle the sugar and bitters together until cube is mostly dissolved. Add whiskey and fill with ice. Garnish with lemon peel.

and poets of the early 1900s, it was thought to inspire a sort of deep, dark creativity.

Absinthe itself is somewhat mysterious. It is a distilled spirit brewed with herbs and bark—particularly wormwood, which is the main ingredient accused of causing toxic reactions. The liquor looks green or yellowish or clear in the bottle, depending on which kind you choose, yet it turns a milky off-white when water is added. It smells herby and tastes a bit like black licorice. The best absinthe is made in France, although some comes from Eastern Europe.

Laws regarding controlled substances (such as hallucinogens) are still in effect. So why is absinthe legal again? It has been determined that thujone, a substance derived from wormwood, is not as toxic as once believed.

VERMOUTH

Vermouth makes for a wonderful aperitif on its own and adds complexity to a cocktail when used as a modifier. Essentially wine steeped in herbs, sweet vermouth is red in color and, as the name implies, slightly sweet. I like it on the rocks with a twist of orange, but it is more commonly used in classic cocktails such as the Manhattan, Negroni, and Blood and Sand. Dry vermouth looks like white wine and sometimes has a slightly caramel hue. It also is great over ice with a twist of lemon, and it is used in equal parts with gin in a classic martini.

LIQUEURS

Fruit cordials and cream-based liqueurs come in a rainbow of flavors and sometimes can be substituted for the simple syrup in a cocktail recipe, adding an extra burst of flavor, color, or texture to the drink. Below I provide a list of selected liqueurs and cordials, some common and others more exotic. Check your local specialty store for other varieties.

APPLE & PEAR: applejack, calvados, apple eau de vie

ORANGE: triple sec, Cointreau, Grand Marnier, Gran Gala

LEMON: lemoncello

BERRIES: Maraschino liqueur (cherry), Cherry Heering; Chambord liqueur (raspberry), Crème de Cassis (black currant), berry brandies

PEACH: peach brandies, schnapps

GINGER: Domaine de Canton, Elixir G

FLOWERS: St. Germain Elderflower liqueur, Crème de Violette

COFFEE: Kahlua, Café Boheme, Starbucks coffee and crème

TEA: Zen Green Tea lIqueur, Chai Voyant

NUTS: Amaretto (almond), Frangelico (hazelnuts)

MELON: Midori (honeydew)

LICORICE: Anis, Absinthe, Sambuca

CHOCOLATE: Godiva white and dark chocolate cream liqueurs, crème de cacao (white or dark)

MINT: Crème de menthe (green and white), Peppermint schnapps

ECO-FRIENDLY AND ORGANIC SPIRITS
One of my favorite classes to teach is The Liquid Muse Sustainable Sips. The topic of sustainable cocktails has excited my students in cities such as Seattle, Los Angeles, Chicago,

Boston, and New York, proving that people in all corners of the country want to make healthier choices, even when it comes to indulgence. "Going green" is a growing trend worldwide, and eco-friendly philosophies can easily be incorporated into every aspect of our lives. One of my catchphrases is "Eat organic? Drink organic!" After all, why would you put so much effort into finding environmentally friendly food for your plate but not apply the same effort toward what goes into your glass?

Growing numbers of "certified organic" spirits and wines are hitting shelves in both small and large stores. Some are made by mom-and-pop-style artisanal distilleries, whereas others are being rolled out by some of the largest liquor companies in existence. Organic products generally cost a bit more than the average bottle, but for those looking to incorporate the "green" lifestyle into every aspect of their lives, it is worth the extra cash. Don't forget to also use fresh organic juices, fruits, and herbs in your Sustainable Sips®!

MIX UP SOME FUN!

The first thing I stress when teaching The Liquid Muse cocktail classes is to relax, because cocktails are fun! Don't get worried about what's right or wrong, good or bad. If you like it, it's right. That being said, it's always wise to start with the basics before getting too experimental. Pretty soon, you'll be shaking and stirring with confidence.

If you're new at creating cocktails, start by simply taking a drink you already love and switching out or adding a few ingredients. Love mojitos? Try using Pisco or vodka instead of rum and adding some raspberries. Are you crazy about lemon drops? Use lemon-flavored shochu instead of vodka and add a little ginger-infused simple syrup to sweeten it. Once you customize a few standard drinks, you will want to try all kinds of combinations.

Dale DeGroff is known as the King of Cocktails, and most of us who work as professional mixologists look to him as the last word in all things cocktailian. In one of the many seminars I've taken with him over the years, I made note of this formula he presented: 1½ ounces spirit, 1 ounce simple syrup, ¾ ounce lemon or lime juice. If you want to make a true cocktail by definition, as described earlier in this chapter, eliminate the citrus and add a dash of bitters and water in some form. Have fun!

Part 3

Champagne: The Bubbly Basics

Now that the question has been popped, corks will be a-popping, too! Champagne is part of any major celebration—and has an especially important role in weddings. From the proposal to the wedding day, saying "I do" will likely involve a flowing stream of tiny bubbles.

Marilyn Monroe is rumored to have loved champagne so much that she bathed in it. Scrub-a-dub-bubbly!

You don't need to be a sommelier to pick the right sparkling wine for your special day. By the end of this chapter, you'll have a few bubbly basics under your belt so you can choose which sparkling wine will add sizzling sophistication to your upcoming celebrations.

What Is Champagne, Anyway?

Champagne is essentially carbonated white wine, although not all carbonated white wine is champagne. In order to be true champagne, the contents of the bottle must come from a region in France called Champagne. Period. This is because Champagne is an AOC (*Appellation d'Origine Contrôlée*), which is kind of like a trademark stamp on products from that particular region.

Other countries have their own AOC regions, too. For example, Cava comes primarily from the Penedès region in Catalonia, Spain. Prosecco is made from its namesake grape, grown mainly around Veneto, Italy. Think of it like eating a "Dodger Dog." This fan favorite falls into the general hot dog category, but you know a Dodger Dog comes specifically from a baseball game at Dodger Stadium in Los Angeles.

In the United States we don't have a specific AOC for bubbly, so our generic term is simply *sparkling wine*. However, we also tend to use the word *champagne* as a blanket term for all sparkling wines and cocktails made from them (i.e., "champagne cocktails"), even if it is not technically correct. For our purposes in this book, that is fine. I may use "champagne" and "sparkling wine" interchangeably in the cocktail recipes.

Is More Expensive Champagne Better?

Don't be convinced that spending more money means you are getting a better bubbly. There are some fabulous sparklers (and noncarbonated wines) in stores for under $10 per bottle. Particularly when making cocktails (mixing champagne with juices, etc.), you don't need a pricey product. In fact, I'd advise against it. Why spend extra cash on high-priced champagne only to dilute it with ingredients that mess with the flavor? Just remember The Liquid Muse Rule #1 when it comes to any kind of wine: There is no wrong answer. If you like it, it's good, plain and simple.

Sweet or Dry?

The word *spumante* directly translates to "foaming" in Italian. In the United States we tend to identify spumante with sweeter sparkling wine (such as Asti Spumante). However, not all Italian spumante wines are sweet. "Brut" or "Extra Brut" means that the sparkling wine is dry or extra dry, respectively (dry=less sweet).

Does Size Matter?

Unlike diamonds, ladies, when it comes to bubbles, it is believed that smaller is better. Tiny bubbles travel to the surface of your glass more quickly than larger ones, resulting in a bouquet of aroma as they burst just beneath the tip of your nose or coat your tongue with flavor as they pop on its surface.

Size and quality also reveal much about the way the bubbles got there in the first place. For example, *methode champenoise* means that the bubbles occur naturally via fermentation pre- and post-bottling. This is usually considered the highest-quality fermentation method and produces tiny bubbles. Another way of turning wine bubbly is to inject it with carbon dioxide, as is done with soft drinks. These bubbles are usually larger and move more slowly.

When a bottle has the term *frizzante* on the label, the wine is only slightly bubbly. For example, Vinho Verde is a lightly carbonated Portuguese sparkling wine, sometimes referred to as semi-sparkling because it has very low levels of carbon dioxide.

My husband snuck a bottle of expensive bubbly into his suitcase and surprised me with it when we arrived in Hawaii for our honeymoon. Why not surprise your new hubby with a bottle of special champagne?

Tickled Pink

The juice squeezed from pretty much any grape is more or less translucent. The pink or red color in wine occurs when that juice is allowed to ferment with the skins from dark-colored grapes. This can affect the taste of the product to a certain extent and, of course, its appearance.

Rosé champagnes, like nonsparkling rosé wine, can be sickly sweet or bone dry. Some people think that the "pink stuff" is of lesser quality, but that is not always true. In fact, sparkling rosé has been popular in Europe for eons and is becoming a big trend in the United States! The drier rosés tend to be better, so go to your local wine shop or liquor store and take home a few to sample. (You owe it to yourself to indulge in a little effervescent experimentation . . .)

Turning Red

Lambrusco is an Italian red wine with a seductively light effervescence. Italian Brachetto and French Braquet are bubbly reds from the Mediterranean region. Most of us are familiar with Australian shiraz (the same grape is called syrah elsewhere). But did you know that this wildly popular robust red wine also comes in sparkling form? Just one more treat bubbling up from Down Under!

The Vessel

Champagne is usually served in one of two glasses: the more modern tubular champagne flute or the old-fashioned round, bowl-shaped champagne coupe. While most people use the flute nowadays, claiming that the tube shape preserves the wine's effervescence, I personally love the coupe because it screams of old-world glamour. (With the resurgence of classic cocktails, anything grandma and grandpa drank—or what they drank it in—is totally hip!) Here's a hint: I've found some of my favorite antique glassware, including champagne coupes, in vintage stores and at Goodwill for pennies on the dollar.

The original mold for the Champagne Coupe was made from the breast of Queen Marie Antoinette of France. Incidentally, she loved champagne and the "high life." Maybe that's why she is famous for declaring, "Let them eat cake!" when told that poor French peasants had no bread. (Little wonder she was beheaded during the French Revolution . . .)

Part 4

Love & Libations: The Recipes

1
IT'S OFFICIAL!

This chapter begins with a "pop," as any celebratory gathering should. From there we journey, one cocktail at a time, toward the joyful march down the aisle. The drinks on the coming pages are easy to prepare yet transform a run-of-the-mill party into a cocktailian extravaganza.

POP THE CORK!

Champagne can bring extra "sparkle" to your wedding in a myriad of ways. Why not consider a sparkling *cocktail* rather than just plain bubbly for the champagne toast at your wedding? Or perhaps you could greet guests with an elegant refreshment as they arrive for the ceremony. From bridal shower to honeymoon, I predict a sea of sparkling wine in your future.

Whether you choose a classic recipe or go for something a bit more creative, your guests will remember the unique addition of a champagne cocktail to a traditional moment. If you're truly bold, refer to the Create Your Own Signature Cocktail chapter in this book to design a drink that no one has ever tasted before. You could even invite your bridal party over to test the recipes you devise. (There's always an excuse for a party of some kind during this special wedding-planning time!)

CLASSIC CHAMPAGNE COCKTAIL

(Champagne Flute)

The first champagne cocktail recipe dates back over 200 years. Here, as in any true cocktail, bitters are an integral ingredient. I love using a dry champagne for this drink because the sugar sweetens it slightly. Twist the lemon twirl above the drink so the rind will lightly mist the rim with natural citrus oil.

1 sugar cube

Healthy dash Angostura bitters

4 ounces chilled champagne

1 lemon twirl

Place the sugar cube in the bottom of a champagne flute, and douse it with bitters. Slowly fill the glass with ice-cold champagne. Garnish with a lemon twirl.

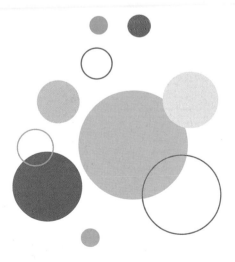

FRENCH 75
(Champagne Flute)

This classic bubbly drink has a kick of juniper from the gin. It is supposedly named after a gun used in World War I, and some say the drink was originally made with cognac. Why not try it both ways to decide which you like better?

1 ounce gin

¼ ounce lemon juice

½ ounce simple syrup, page 9

4 ounces chilled champagne

1 lemon twirl

Shake gin, lemon juice, and simple syrup with ice. Strain into a champagne flute. Top with champagne. Garnish with a lemon twirl.

VANILLA BLUSH
(Champagne Flute)

This recipe comes courtesy of Charlotte Voisey, who was named the United Kingdom's Bartender of the Year in 2005. She is currently the master mixologist at William Grant and Sons USA, and happens to be one of the loveliest lasses in the liquor industry. This cocktail is strong and sweet with a feminine touch.

3 fresh strawberries heavily dusted in vanilla sugar

1 ounce cognac

3 ounces chilled champagne

Muddle strawberries and vanilla sugar in the bottom of a mixing glass. Add cognac and ice. Shake well, then strain into a champagne flute. Top with champagne.

♟ BOUQUET OF ROSÉ
(Champagne Coupe)

This champagne cocktail is simple, elegant, and dripping with romance. I designed it for the launch of Napa's Domaine Carneros Brut Rosé (Taittinger Champagne). I took my cue from the light fruit aromas inherent to this bubbly, and layered them with the softly feminine floral influence of roses.

Spritz rose water
½ ounce rose-infused simple syrup, page 9
3½ ounces sparkling rosé
1 sprig fresh lavender

Spritz a chilled champagne coupe with rose water. Pour in rose-infused simple syrup and sparkling rosé. Lay a sprig of fresh lavender across the top of the glass as an aromatic garnish.

RING-A-DING-TINI
(Champagne Flute)

I designed this drink as Pinky vodka's holiday cocktail, pulling my favorite elements from both the Bellini and the classic champagne cocktail. The açaí juice adds some tart fruit notes, while the peach puree sweetly softens the edges. Meanwhile, the earthy notes are amped up with a dash of rhubarb bitters.

1 sugar cube

Dash Fee Brothers rhubarb bitters

1 ounce Pinky vodka

½ ounce peach or passion fruit puree

¾ ounce açaí juice

¼ ounce simple syrup, page 9

2½ ounces chilled champagne

Muddle the sugar cube and rhubarb bitters in the bottom of a mixing glass. Add Pinky vodka, fruit puree, açaí juice, simple syrup, and ice. Shake well, then strain into a chilled champagne flute. Top with ice-cold champagne.

BUBBLY BEIJO
(Champagne Flute)

When creating this drink, I decided to soften the spicy kick in the ginger liqueur with sweet agave nectar and herby cilantro. It is a change of pace, for sure!

　4–5 cilantro leaves

　1 ounce Domaine de Canton ginger liqueur

　¾ ounce cachaça

　¾ ounce mandarin orange juice

　¼ ounce agave nectar

　3 ounces chilled champagne

Muddle cilantro in the bottom of a mixing glass. Add ginger liqueur, cachaça, mandarin orange juice, and agave nectar. Shake and strain into a chilled champagne flute. Top with champagne.

❗ BELLINI
(Champagne Flute)

This classic drink was created by Giuseppi Cipriani in 1948, at Harry's Bar in Venice, Italy. It recently celebrated its 60th anniversary. (Let's toast to your marriage hitting that milestone!)

1½ ounces homemade white peach puree*
4 ounces prosecco

Pour the peach puree and 2 ounces of prosecco into a mixing glass with ice. Cover with the cocktail shaker tin or lid. Instead of shaking vigorously, "roll" the mixture back and forth a few times to blend it. Then strain it into a champagne flute. Top with the remaining prosecco and serve. In summer, when peaches are readily available, you can garnish this drink with a slice of fresh peach.

*THE LIQUID MUSE HOMEMADE WHITE PEACH PUREE: In a small saucepan over low heat, stir 1 cup peeled, chopped peaches with 1 ounce fresh lemon juice, ½ cup sugar, and ¼ cup water for 10 minutes. Let cool, then pour mixture into a blender and puree it. Using a kitchen strainer, strain that mixture into a plastic bottle and store it in the refrigerator for up to 2 days.

The Liquid Muse Mixology Tip:
Add a splash of apricot brandy to "float" on the top of the drink for extra pizzazz.

❢ LEMON ROSE BELLINI
(Champagne Flute)

This recipe is from fellow champagne lover and female mixologist Kim Haasarud of Liquid Architecture; it appears in her book *101 Champagne Cocktails* (John Wiley & Sons, 2008). This colorful cocktail has a playful twist—wonderful for a bridal shower, engagement party, or even during the cocktail hour preceding dinner at a summer wedding reception.

> **1 spoonful lemon sorbet, softened**
> **½ ounce citrus vodka (optional)**
> **4 ounces sparkling rosé**
> **2–3 raspberries**

Combine the sorbet with the citrus vodka in a cocktail shaker with ice. Shake vigorously and add the sparkling rosé. Stir. Strain into a chilled champagne flute. Garnish with raspberries.

▼ LAMBRUSCO ROSEMARY FIZZ

(Champagne Coupe)

Drinking a sparkling red Lambrusco wine reminds me of childhood summers with my family in the south of France. Italy is about half an hour from Beaulieu-sur-Mer, where my dad is from, so Italian wines, liqueurs, and spirits were some of the first ones I tasted. Moreover, rosemary flourishes in the Mediterranean and is a popular herb in local dishes. I couldn't help but feel a little nostalgic when creating this drink.

1 orange wheel

3–4 fresh rosemary leaves

¾ ounce Grand Marnier

4 ounces sparkling Lambrusco

1 sprig fresh rosemary

Muddle orange wheel and rosemary leaves in the bottom of mixing glass. Add Grand Marnier and shake with ice. Strain into a champagne coupe. Top with Lambrusco. Garnish with a sprig of fresh rosemary.

The Liquid Muse Mixology Tip:
Setting an aromatic garnish on the edge of a glass is an elegant way to subtly enhance the natural aromas of a drink without interfering with the flavor.

FLORAL FIG

(Champagne Flute)

The inspiration for this drink came from my own back yard in Los Angeles. When figs were in season and I had eaten my fill, I found ways to incorporate them into my cocktails by creating a fig puree! (Figs from the supermarket or a premade puree can work just as well.) This drink can be sipped as an aperitif but is equally nice—maybe even better—as a dessert when served with a hard, dry cheese (such as a Spanish Manchego).

Granulated sugar

1 ounce fig puree

¾ ounce elderflower syrup or liqueur

3½ ounces chilled champagne

Rim a champagne flute with sugar and set aside. Shake fig puree and elderflower liqueur with ice. Pour through a small kitchen strainer into the champagne flute. Top with champagne.

NOLITA HEAT
(Champagne Flute)

I was honored to have this creation debut in 2008 as the "First Official Nonalcoholic Cocktail" at Tales of the Cocktail, one of the most prestigious cocktail conferences in the world. I named it the NOLitA Heat for two reasons: Tales of the Cocktail takes place in New Orleans in the summertime (when the temperature soars), and the spicy jalapeño heats up your taste buds!

2 jalapeño slices

½ ounce lime juice

3 ounces mango juice

1 ounce prickly pear puree (available in bar stores and online)

Fre alcohol-removed Brut

1 skewered whole jalapeño or Thai chili

Muddle jalapeño slices and lime juice in a mixing glass. Add ice and mango juice, then shake vigorously. Strain into a champagne flute. Slowly pour in Prickly Pear puree, allowing it to settle on the bottom of the glass. Top with nonalcoholic sparkling wine, and garnish with a skewered jalapeño or Thai chili on the side of the glass.

THE ENGAGEMENT PARTY

An engagement party is probably the first celebration of many over the coming months. It is a great opportunity for you to show off your new ring (and beaming smile) while your guy gets pats on the back, and a little ribbing, from his buddies. If your parents haven't met his by now, this is also a good first step toward bringing the families together. And it's an opportunity for all of your friends to meet, which will make the wedding more fun for everyone. (It might even be the perfect time for you to play matchmaker and introduce that fab girlfriend of yours to your fiancé's very eligible buddy . . . with less pressure than the actual wedding day.)

Your engagement party may be casual or formal, large or small, thrown in a fancy venue or in someone's backyard. What's important is that you add a few touches that reflect both of your personalities so each partner's loved ones start to get an idea of why you fit together so well. Bring out family photo albums, make a playlist of your favorites tunes, and choose food and drink that reflect your cultures so everyone can get to know you both a little bit better.

Request that each guest at your engagement party (and everyone invited to your wedding) fill out a recipe card with his or her favorite cocktail. Print all the recipes in a booklet to use as a giveaway at your wedding reception. It is a one-of-a-kind souvenir all your guests will treasure.

▼ A NEW DAWN
(Rocks Glass)

You're about to start a new life, as a new wife. Sounds like a new dawn is on your horizon. Vermouth and gin have been considered a natural pairing ever since the original martini was invented. I love grapefruit juice in this kind of drink because it adds a little citrus without becoming too sweet. If your celebration takes place in the summer, use a tall glass filled with ice and add a little more soda.

1½ ounces sweet vermouth

½ ounce gin

3 ounces freshly squeezed grapefruit juice

Splash grapefruit soda

1 maraschino cherry

Pour sweet vermouth, gin, and grapefruit juice into an ice-filled rocks glass. Top with a splash of grapefruit soda and stir. Garnish with a maraschino cherry.

"Look for a photographer with a creative eye, and you'll be the most pleased with photos. So many people end up with the same traditional, formal photographs, so look for a photographer's whose work is unique and not run-of-the-mill."

–Moshe B. Zusman, Photographer, Washington DC

▼ THE SWEETHEART COCKTAIL

(Martini Glass)

This cocktail looks like a valentine with its layers of red, pink, and white, and its silky texture makes it a sensual sipping experience. The Campari has a bitter flavor that is balanced by the tart lemon and sweet grenadine. The egg white makes the drink velvety and creates a slight foam on its surface.

1½ ounces Pinky vodka

1 ounce simple syrup, page 9

¾ ounce lemon juice

¼ ounce Campari

1 small egg white

¼ ounce grenadine

Pour all ingredients except grenadine into a mixing glass. Dry shake for a few seconds. Fill with ice and shake vigorously for at least 30 seconds to make the egg white frothy. Strain into a chilled martini glass. Slowly drizzle grenadine into the cocktail, allowing it to settle at the bottom of the glass, creating a layered effect.

♈ GOLDEN KIWI MARGARITA
(Margarita Glass)

The margarita is the number one cocktail in the world. By substituting Gran Gala for triple sec, this version takes on more layers of flavor. And using agave nectar with a 100% agave tequila is a no-brainer. The golden kiwi makes the drink more exotic, but if you don't find this variety in your local market, a green kiwi is fine.

2 slices golden kiwi, ¼-inch thick

2 ounces reposado tequila

¾ ounce Gran Gala orange liqueur

¾ ounce agave nectar

1 ounce lime juice

Muddle golden kiwi in the bottom of a mixing glass. Add tequila, Gran Gala, agave nectar, and lime juice. Shake well and strain into a chilled cocktail glass. Can be served straight up or on the rocks.

One of the first things you will do after you've told your parents you're betrothed is choose your maid of honor. If you don't live in the same city, send her a special package asking her to play that special role—a message in a bottle, a silver-plated liquor flask engraved with a mysterious future date, or a piece of jewelry to wear for the wedding.

GETTING COZY WITH THE IN-LAWS

Meeting the parents, siblings, aunts, uncles, and cousins can be a little intimidating—especially if your fiancé has a big family. If you live in the same town, break the ice by inviting them over for dinner and drinks, in small groups, so you get a chance to know them before the wedding. If you are in different cities, start a wedding blog and invite family members from both sides to contribute.

When it comes to your wedding, both your mom and your fiancé's mom will want to be involved. How do you find that delicate balance of allowing them in without allowing them to take over? Give them each one important thing to be in charge of: selecting the hotel for out-of-town guests or choosing the table centerpieces. They want to help, so let them! You will have enough to do.

"The quickest way to get what you want is to help others get what they want. Be a loving, kind, generous, openhearted, sensitive person, and the world will reflect that back to you—even in the form of your mother-in-law—and she may just surprise you and turn out to be an ally and a friend!"

–Sally Shields, author of *The Daughter-in-Law Rules: 101 Surefire Ways to Manage (and Make Friends with) Your Mother-in-Law!*

Y THE MOTHER-IN-LAW COSMO

(Martini Glass)

Your new mother-in-law probably wants to be accepted by you as much as you want to be accepted by her. After all, you are the new #1 woman in her son's life. You may already know each other well and be great friends before the wedding. Or you may be cautious strangers. Either way, it behooves you to make a friendly advance. What better way to break the ice than to shake it up along with a little liquor? If your future mother-in-law doesn't drink, make a nonalcoholic cocktail just for her. She will appreciate your thoughtfulness, and the gesture will give you both a chance to bond.

My mother-in-law loves Cosmopolitans. She has a particular way of making them—more tart than sweet—which I also like, so right off the bat we had something in common beyond her son. Sip one (or three) of these with *your* future mother-in-law!

1½ ounces citrus vodka

1 ounce lime juice

¾ ounce Cointreau

2 ounces cranberry juice

1 lime wedge

Shake all ingredients with ice. Strain into a martini glass. Garnish with a lime wedge on the rim of the glass.

♀ THE ROYAL TIPPLE

(Wine Glass)

Your mom shares in your special day—and has probably dreamt of it as long as you have. Celebrate her opportunity to walk down the aisle as the Mother of the Bride, but don't forget that she is about to become your husband's mother-in-law, too. You can facilitate their relationship by avoiding the temptation to complain about your new husband to your mom when you and your beloved get into an argument. My mom—a wise woman who manages to give good advice while remaining neutral—enjoys a before-dinner drink from time to time. It is rumored that the Queen of England likes a Dubonnet and gin aperitif. Given that my mom is English and likes Dubonnet, I designed this wine-based cocktail in her honor.

3 ounces Dubonnet
½ ounce gin
¼ ounce lemon juice
¼ ounce simple syrup, page 9
1 white rose

Shake all liquid ingredients with ice and strain into a wine glass filled with fresh ice. Present it to your mom with a single white rose.

♈ THICKER THAN WATER
(Martini Glass)

At our wedding, every person in our immediate families walked down the aisle. Our three sisters, his grandma, and all four of our parents made the wedding march a true family affair! Try to incorporate your new brothers and sisters into the wedding ceremony so that everyone feels like part of the celebration. Toast the expansion of both of your families into one happy group with this unique combination of fresh fruit juices with South of the Border flair.

> 1½ ounces tequila
> ¾ ounce Cherry Heering liqueur
> ¾ ounce orange juice
> ½ ounce lime juice
> ½ ounce agave nectar

Pour all ingredients into a mixing glass and shake well with ice. Strain into a martini glass.

☙ PRENUP PUNCH
(Wine Glass)

No matter how much you love your fiancé, you may have a legal matter on your mind. Some people consider a prenuptial agreement unromantic; however, it is not uncommon to approach your marriage license (a lawfully binding contract) the way you would a business agreement. If you decide to move forward with a prenup, then toast to never having to use it.

A traditional punch, according to cocktail historian David Wondrich, is made of sugar, bitters or spices, lemon, water, and a high-proof spirit. This drink has those elements in a single-serving format.

1½ ounces pear vodka or high proof white rum

¾ ounce wildflower honey–infused simple syrup, page 9

½ teaspoon ground cloves

½ ounce lemon juice

Splash sparkling water

1 edible flower

Shake vodka, honey-infused simple syrup, cloves, and lemon juice with ice. Strain into a wine glass filled with fresh ice. Top with a splash of sparkling water. Float an edible flower on the surface of the drink.

"A prenuptial agreement is the best gift a bride and groom can give each other before their wedding day."

–Jacqueline Harounian, law partner at Wisselman, Harounian & Associates, Great Neck, NY

2
THE NEXT ROUND (OF PRE-PARTIES)

Now that you've had the engagement party, schmoozed the in-laws, and taken care of any remaining legal matters, it's time to kick it up a notch. Let the serious party period begin!

You may have one inclusive bridal shower, bringing together everyone from your college roommate to your granny. Or you may split up the celebrations to fit the dynamics of specific groups of friends. Either way, this period is your last hurrah as a singleton. Live it up and revel in the girl time. You'll have plenty of days and nights ahead to canoodle with the love of your life. Right now, focus on you and the women who've helped shape the person you've become—the one whom your fiancé is about to wed. And don't forget that he'll have his own night out with the boys. If you want to give your groom killer cocktails to enjoy with his buddies, skip to the end of this chapter.

BACHELORETTE PARTY SHOTS

Let's face it: The bachelorette party is probably the one wedding-related event where you can get a little wild. When you and your girls hit the town, you may decide to go high brow, or you may hit every dive bar from Mississippi to Michigan. Whatever kind of party you have, one thing is for sure—you'll want to double check the photos in your cell phone before you get home.

This collection of shots is easy to make at home and simple enough to ask any bartender to make for you. Be warned—they may be only 1 ounce each, but they can sneak up on you!

▇ THE MALE STRIPPER MADE ME SIN

(Shot Glass)

In case things get a little "hot" during your bachelorette party, this shot can be your excuse.

½ ounce vodka

¼ ounce cinnamon schnapps

¼ ounce cream

3 red hots

Pour vodka, schnapps, and cream into a shot glass. Drop three red hots into the bottom of the glass.

CRY FOR FREEDOM
(Shot Glass)

Some brides get cold feet right before the wedding. If you see a loss of freedom flashing before your eyes, just remember all the bad dates you've been on in the past.

Salt
½ ounce tequila
¼ ounce triple sec
¼ ounce lime juice

Rim a shot glass with salt. Pour in tequila, triple sec, and lime juice.

BALL AND CHAIN
(Shot Glass)

With the right person, marital constraints can be a good thing!

½ ounce whiskey
¼ ounce lemon vodka
¼ ounce maple syrup
1 lemon twist

Pour whiskey, vodka, and maple syrup into a shot glass. Rub rim of glass with lemon twist.

■ (ALMOST) BAREFOOT AND PREGNANT
(Shot Glass)

No need to rush into this one—but if it's on your agenda, have plenty of fun before it happens!

½ ounce orange-flavored vodka
¼ ounce orange curaçao
¼ ounce white chocolate liqueur

Pour all three ingredients into a shot glass.

■ ROSEBUD
(Shot Glass)

For you romantic girls, this sweet shot is the perfect girly drink.

Graham cracker crumbs
Pinch cinnamon
½ ounce vodka
¼ ounce grenadine
¼ ounce Starbuck's cream liqueur

Rim a shot glass with graham cracker crumbs ground with a pinch of cinnamon in a food processor. Pour vodka, grenadine, then cream liqueur, in that order, into the shot glass for a layered effect.

BRIDAL SHOWER PUNCHES

As much as the wedding will be about you and your groom, the process of planning it is very much about you and your girlfriends. Your best gal pals, your sisters, and your mom will be your biggest allies during this exciting, stressful, wonderful time. They will listen to every concern, share your enthusiasm, get giddy over the perfect pair of shoes, and scrutinize every tiny little detail like no guy can (or wants to).

Your husband is the person you'll spend the rest of your life with, but your girlfriends loved you before you even knew he existed. With that in mind, try to make the bridal shower as much fun for them as it is for you. Start by creating some memories over delicious cocktails!

Depending on the kind of shower you have, you may be able to hire a bartender to shake up individual drinks for each person on demand. If not, opt for one of these two punches so each guest can serve herself.

The Liquid Muse Mixology Tip:
Before modern refrigeration and ice cube makers, old-time bartenders had to carve or chip ice from large blocks. One big block of ice is ideal for chilling a punch, as it will keep the liquid cold but melt more slowly than ice cubes. Make one by filling a small plastic tub (the kind spreadable margarine comes in) with water and freezing it overnight. Or use a Bundt pan to make an ice wreath. You can freeze berries or sliced fruit into either for colorful flair.

OTOÑO ROJO SANGRIA

(Makes approximately 12 servings)

Adding a little Spanish flair breathes life into a fiesta anytime of year.
I developed this recipe for Sutter Home's specialty wine called Red. This
sangria is easy to prepare ahead of time and is equally festive in a punch
bowl or a pitcher. The name means "red autumn" in Spanish, and this
punch's nutty layers and warm, earthy notes make it ideal for late summer
through winter. You can even serve it as a stovetop-mulled wine punch for
a winter wedding!

½ cup raw sugar

½ cup water

1 cup brandy

2 oranges, each cut into 8 pieces, peels on

½ cup whole peeled almonds

3 whole cloves

1 750-milliliter bottle Sutter Home Red

1 orange and 1 lemon, sliced into wheels

Dissolve sugar and water in medium-size saucepan. Bring to
a boil, stirring constantly. Reduce heat to low and add brandy,
orange pieces, almonds, and cloves. Simmer for 8 to 10
minutes, stirring occasionally. Remove from heat and place in
refrigerator for at least 30 minutes to cool.

Strain mixture into a large punch bowl. Discard cooked
fruit, almonds, and cloves. Add bottle of Sutter Home Red to
brandy mixture. Float orange and lemon wheels on the surface
of the sangria for garnish.

MISS CHARMING'S GARDEN PARTY PUNCH

(Makes 20-25 servings)

This punch recipe and beautiful ice bowl come from mixologist Cheryl Charming (aka Miss Charming™), who has authored nine bartending books, including *Knack Bartending Basics: More than 400 Classic and Contemporary Cocktails for Any Occasion.* One of the clever things about this beautiful presentation is that the bowl keeps the punch cold. The sweet, floral elderflower liqueur and flowery appearance make it a lovely addition to a spring wedding.

1 750-milliliter bottle St-Germain elderflower liqueur

1 750-milliliter bottle pear vodka

1 flowered ice bowl mold*

4 bottles chilled brut champagne

Mix the liqueur and vodka together in a pitcher. Chill in the fridge. When ready to serve, divide the pitcher mixture into four equal parts. Pour one into the flowered ice bowl and top with a chilled bottle of champagne. Replenish as needed, using this ratio.

*FLOWERED ICE BOWL MOLD: Start with two large plastic bowls, one slightly smaller so it can fit inside the other. Fill the larger bowl halfway with water. (More can be added later, if necessary.) Place the smaller bowl inside the larger one, allowing the water to come up the sides. Slip flowers into the water in between the two bowls, then add weight to the inner, smaller bowl to keep it in place. Tape the bowls together, then freeze them overnight. When you're ready to serve your punch, thaw the bowls for 15 minutes and the molds will pop off.

BRIDAL LUNCHEON LIBATIONS

Some brides have more than one bridal shower, and some throw a luncheon for their gal pals the day before the wedding. This event is a chance for out-of-town friends and relatives to have some special "girl time" with you. It is also yet another opportunity for a group of guests to get to know each before the wedding reception. The bridal party luncheon is a more ladylike affair than the bachelorette party, as moms and grandmas may be involved. These cocktails go nicely with an afternoon tea or midday meal and also provide single-serving cocktail options for your bridal shower(s).

▼ THYME FOR ROMANCE
(Cocktail Glass)

This cocktail is made in a classic style and with Bols genever, a re-released herbal gin predecessor from a centuries-old recipe. Give it a try!

½-inch piece fresh ginger

1½ ounces Bols genever

1 ounce thyme-infused simple syrup, page 9

¾ ounce lime juice

Dash Angostura bitters

1 sprig fresh thyme

Muddle ginger in the bottom of a mixing glass. Add Bols genever, simple syrup, lime juice, bitters, and ice. Shake and strain into a small cocktail glass. Garnish with a sprig of thyme.

▼ MALVINA COCKTAIL
(Martini Glass)

Christine D'Abrosca is a San Francisco–based mixologist with a particular fondness for tequila. This recipe, one of her originals, brings out the tequila lover in all of us.

Granulated sugar
Ground cinnamon
1¾ ounces añejo tequila
¾ ounce lemon juice
¾ ounce Licor 43
½ ounce agave nectar
¼ ounce Cointreau

Rim a martini glass with a mixture of granulated sugar and ground cinnamon. Set aside. Pour all other ingredients into a mixing glass with ice and shake well. Gently strain into the martini glass.

♉ WHITE POMEGRANATE TEANI
(Martini Glass)

Tea is a growing trend on cocktail menus everywhere. White tea is the newest rage among tea aficionados, but you can use chamomile if you prefer.

1½ ounces mandarin vodka

1 ounce white tea-infused simple syrup, page 9

½ ounce pomegranate juice

½ ounce lemon juice

White tea-pomegranate ice cubes*

Splash sparkling white jasmine tea (or citrus-flavored sparkling water)

Shake vodka, tea-infused simple syrup, and juices with ice. Strain into a martini glass. Add 3 white tea–pomegranate ice cubes. Top with sparkling jasmine tea.

*WHITE TEA–POMEGRANATE ICE CUBES: Pour 1 cup white tea into an ice cube tray. Add 3–5 pomegranate seeds to each cube. Freeze overnight.

▼ BLUSHING BRIDE

(Wine Glass)

I developed several versions of this recipe, and this formula is my favorite. Wine cocktails are a fun and unique way to experiment behind your home bar, and they give wine lovers a new way to think about enjoying their favorite beverage.

1 heaping tablespoon diced strawberries

1 tablespoon torn basil

1 ounce strawberry syrup (or strawberry liqueur)

¼ ounce freshly squeezed lemon juice

2 ounces rosé wine

Pinch freshly ground black pepper

Splash soda water

1 whole strawberry

Muddle diced strawberries and torn basil in the bottom of a tall glass. Add the strawberry syrup through pepper and shake with ice. Strain into a wine glass and add a splash of soda water. Garnish with a whole strawberry on the side of the glass.

SPARKLING SOUTHERN BELLE
(Champagne Flute)

The feminine lilt to a southern accent suggests genteel elegance and charm. But don't be fooled—southern girls love a good drink. Bourbon, aka "America's Spirit," comes from their neck of the woods. I've incorporated it into a champagne cocktail to give a southern peach her due!

2 tablespoons sugar

1 ounce peach puree, page 46

1 ounce bourbon

Dash peach bitters (or Angostura bitters)

3 ounces chilled champagne

Splash apricot brandy or peach liqueur

Rim a champagne flute with sugar. Set aside. Pour peach puree, bourbon, and bitters into a mixing glass. Fill with ice and shake well. Gently strain into the sugar-rimmed flute, then add champagne and top with a splash of apricot brandy or peach liqueur.

"The latest name-change trend is the bride taking her maiden name as her middle name. This option allows the best of both worlds: She can take her husband's name and keep her maiden name without the mouthful of hyphenation."

–Danielle Tate, founder of MissNowMrs.com

BATTLING BRIDEZILLA

No matter how stressed you feel about wedding details, don't forget that everyone is working on your behalf. Show your appreciation by keeping your cool, and show your class by being diplomatic whenever possible. Just in case you need a little liquid help, these drinks have been created especially for the lovely lady whose bridezilla is showing.

LA BRUJA
(Highball Glass)

Bruja means "witch" in Spanish. I'm not trying to imply that a bridezilla is a witch (or anything that rhymes with it); I'm just encouraging the bride-gone-wild to take a moment to regroup with this delicious cocktail created by Damian Windsor, an L.A.–based brand ambassador for Partida Tequila.

1½ ounces Partida reposado tequila

½ ounce lime juice

½ ounce simple syrup, page 9

½ ounce pineapple juice

1 teaspoon freshly grated ginger

¼ ounce egg white

1 ounce ginger ale

1 slice fresh ginger

Omitting the ginger ale, shake all ingredients once without ice and again with ice. Strain into an ice-filled highball glass. Add ginger ale. Stir. Garnish with a slice of fresh ginger.

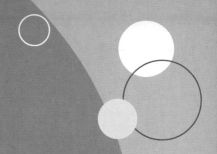

CHILL PILL
(Champagne Flute)

Gwen Sutherland Kaiser pairs astrological insights with cocktails on her blog Intoxicated Zodiac. She uses layers of lavender to maximize the calming effect of this drink (a benefit for women of any sun sign during wedding planning!).

Lavender water (available at health food stores and online)

1 ounce lavender bud–infused vodka*

1 ounce lavender-infused simple syrup, page 9

½ ounce fresh lemon juice

Splash DRY Soda Co. lavender soda

1 sprig lavender or edible flower

Mist the inside of a champagne flute with lavender water and set aside. Shake lavender bud–infused vodka, simple syrup, and lemon juice with ice. Strain into champagne flute and top with lavender soda. Give it a quick stir and present with a sprig of lavender to soothe the senses, or with an edible purple flower.

*LAVENDER BUD–INFUSED VODKA: Infuse 750 milliliters of vodka with 3 cups dried lavender buds (available at health food stores and online). Allow the mixture to sit for several days, then strain.

BOYS' NIGHT OUT

One of the highlights of wedding planning for your man is the bachelor party. And let's be fair: He has sat through countless conversations about flowers, food, decorations, and guest lists, the guy deserves some "dude time." If he has been an eager and willing participant while you obsessed over all those little things he couldn't care less about, give him a free pass to have fun with his buddies before the Big Day.

When thinking about great drinks for your groom-to-be, I decided to reach out to some of my favorite male mixologists, bartenders, and cocktail geeks around the country. These guys are some of the best in the business and have the chops to know what a man-about-town should drink on his big night out. Some of these experts are married, some are single, and one is even in the midst of his own wedding planning as I write this book. So here's a little man-to-man, bro-to-bro imbibing advice. Bottoms up, fellas!

♈ JACKELOPE
(Cocktail Glass)

Derek Brown is a sommelier and mixologist in Washington DC (and a new-lywed to boot). Derek calls this drink "an evolution of the olden-day tipple called the Applejack Rabbit" and adds that the infused maple syrup brings a rich, spicy dimension to his version of a classic.

> 1½ ounces bourbon
>
> ¼ ounce Domaine de Canton ginger liqueur
>
> ¼ ounce American oak–infused maple syrup*
>
> ¼ ounce lemon juice
>
> 2 dashes bitters
>
> 1 orange peel

Shake liquid ingredients and bitters with ice. Strain into a cocktail glass. Garnish with an orange peel.

*AMERICAN OAK–INFUSED MAPLE SYRUP: Add new American oak chips to 100% maple syrup for 48 hours to 3 months, depending on chip size and desired flavor (or use BLiS Bourbon Barrel Matured Maple Syrup for the easy way out).

▼ THE RUSE
(Cocktail Glass)

After shaking his way through Manhattan's exclusive drinking establishments, Eric Alperin has graced many Los Angeles hotspots, including The Varnish, which he and business partner Sasha Petraske own. Eric calls this drink "a play on a recently resurrected classic drink known as the Corpse Reviver." (It may help the groom the morning after his bachelor party, when his corpse may need a little reviving!)

- ¾ ounce gin
- ¾ ounce St-Germain elderflower liqueur
- ¾ ounce Cointreau
- ¾ ounce freshly squeezed lime juice
- 1 bar spoon green Chartreuse
- 1 lime twist

Shake all liquid ingredients with ice. Strain into a chilled cocktail glass. Gently squeeze the lime twist over the surface of the cocktail, peel side down, and serve it with the drink.

"When brides request a part of their reception be designed for their groom, we usually suggest ideas as large as a cigar rolling tent to as small as offering their favorite foods, like a French fry table or sweet tea fountain. The grooms always appreciate the extra effort to include them in the planning."

–Emma Lesesne, Duvall Catering & Event Design, Charleston, SC

▼ THE MAGIC HOUR
(Cocktail Glass)

Ted "Dr. Cocktail" Haigh is a world-renowned cocktail expert and the author of *Vintage Spirits* and *Forgotten Cocktails*. This classic-style drink has a few simple ingredients in perfect balance, bringing a touch of magic at pretty much any hour!

2 ounces Plymouth gin
¾ ounce St-Germain elderflower liqueur
½ ounce fresh lemon juice
1 lemon peel twist

Shake all ingredients well and strain into a stemmed cocktail glass. Garnish with a twist of lemon peel, but do *not* twist the peel over the surface of the drink.

"If you're planning to make a humorous toast, bear in mind that there will probably be a broad cross-section of guests at the reception, some of whom might not appreciate off-color language or risqué stories. Just imagine that your own grandmother is sitting in the front row, and ask yourself if what you're planning to say would offend her."

**–Tom Haibeck, author of *Wedding Toasts Made Easy*
and founder of WeddingToasts.com**

☗ THE REVOLVER
(Cocktail Glass)

Jon Santer is president of the San Francisco chapter of the United States Bartenders' Guild. He created this manly whiskey cocktail in 2001, and it has since shown up on over 500 cocktail lists around the United States and even popped up in New Zealand.

2 ounces Bulliet bourbon
½ ounce Tia Maria
Dash Fee Brothers orange bitters
Dash Regan's orange bitters
1 flamed orange disc

Shake bourbon, Tia Maria, and bitters with ice and strain into a chilled cocktail glass. Garnish with a flamed orange disk.

The Liquid Muse Mixology Tip:
To flame an orange or lemon disc, cut a circular piece of orange peel, removing any fruit (only some white pith and orange peel should remain). Hold the disc between your thumb and forefinger, peel side down, a few inches above the surface of the cocktail. Gently squeeze the edges of the disc while lighting a match in front of it. The oil coming off the peel will momentarily catch fire, creating a burst of flame. Drop the disc into the cocktail and serve.

DIRTY HARRY

(Cocktail Glass)

H. Joseph Ehrmann is the proprietor of Elixir, a historic San Francisco saloon with a "green" emphasis. He calls this drink "a spin on the Lawhill Cocktail with the strength and character to make men feel manly and women swoon, a bit like Dirty Harry himself." In other words, it's a tough-guy drink with enough flavorful finesse from the maraschino liqueur and sweet vermouth to seduce a lady.

¼ ounce absinthe

2 ounces rye whiskey

½ ounce sweet vermouth

¼ ounce maraschino liqueur

1 maraschino cherry

Pour absinthe into a chilled cocktail glass and swirl it around, coating the inside of the glass. Dispose of any extra. Set glass aside. Pour whiskey, sweet vermouth, and maraschino liqueur into an ice-filled mixing glass. Stir well, then strain into the absinthe-coated glass. Garnish with a cherry.

BACHELOR PARTY PUNCH

(Makes 16 man-size servings)

Bobby "G" Gleason is the master mixologist for BeamGlobal Spirits & Wine. His punch recipe makes one big batch of man-strength cocktails for the whole party. The fruit juice may take the edge off the whiskey and rum, but don't be fooled—this recipe packs a punch!

1 liter bottle Jim Beam

1 750-milliliter bottle Cruzan black cherry rum

1 gallon lemonade

20 ounces cranberry or pomegranate juice

Lemon wedges

Pour all ingredients into a large bowl or drink dispenser with a spout. Place one large block of ice in bowl; if you want a cool smoking effect, carefully add several large pieces of dry ice. To serve, stir contents and ladle or pour over ice. Garnish each serving with a wedge of lemon squeezed and dropped in.

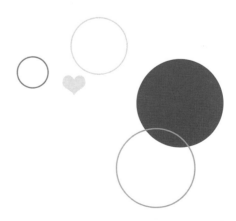

▼ SCOTTISH BREAKFAST

(Rocks Glass)

In addition to writing a cocktail blog featuring witty bartending anecdotes, Jeffrey Morgenthaler is the founder of the Oregon Bartenders Guild and RepealDay.org. I chose his classic-style zesty cocktail to round out this list, as scotch may just be the best late-night breakfast as your cele"bro"tion winds to a close.

1 orange peel

2 ounces scotch

½ ounce Pedro Ximénez sherry

Dash orange bitters

1 large strip orange zest

Rub the inside of a rocks glass with an orange peel until it is coated with the natural oils. Fill the glass with ice and set aside. Pour scotch, Pedro Ximénez, and orange bitters into an ice-filled mixing glass and stir until well chilled. Strain contents into the rocks glass and garnish with orange zest.

3
LOW-CALORIE COCKTAILS

Choosing your dress is one of the most fun parts of wedding planning. You can justify spending hours upon hours browsing through Web sites and catalogues when you're supposed to be working, and who can blame you for spending weekends wandering fancy stores, trying on hundreds of beautiful gowns, veils, and shoes. Essentially, you get to play dress up . . . and this time you get to be the princess, for real.

At the same time, buying a wedding dress can be a bit like swimsuit shopping: You stand in front of the mirror wondering how you'd look 10 pounds thinner. Even if you're already in good shape, the pressure of being the center of attention can send the bride-to-be into a tizzy! First thing: Relax! Your fiancé already loves how you look or he wouldn't have popped the question. Don't fall victim to overly criticizing yourself or obsessive dieting!

That said, there is nothing wrong with looking your absolute best for the happiest day of your life. This chapter provides a few insights into where cocktail calories come from so you can choose wisely when perusing your favorite bar's menu. I also suggest low-calorie cocktails to sip along with your friends while avoiding the calorific little suckers that sabotage your shape-up efforts.

THE COUNTDOWN

When creating low-calorie cocktails, I like to incorporate flavored sparkling water and even the *occasional* diet soda. The idea is to make the drink long and satisfying while using elements of modern mixology and keeping the calorie count as low as possible. You will notice that these cocktails are also low in alcohol, so they are great alternatives when you want to indulge in a drink but not risk getting too tipsy.

COSMO COOLER   Approx 133 Calories
(Tall Glass)

While your girlfriends down the cocktails, you will keep to your diet with this guilt-free indulgence. It tastes like a spritzer version of the original cocktail with far fewer calories.

> **2 ounces cranberry juice**
> **1 ounce citrus vodka**
> **1 ounce lime juice**
> **½ ounce Cointreau**
> **4 ounces lime-flavored sparkling water**
> **1 lime wedge**

Fill a tall glass with ice and pour in all liquid ingredients. Stir with a bar spoon. Garnish with a wedge of lime.

Calorie Counter

VODKA, GIN, TEQUILA, RUM, WHISKEY
= each approximately 73 calories per ounce

LIQUEURS
= approximately 120–150 calories per ounce

TABLE WINE (WHITE)
= approximately 23 calories per ounce

TABLE WINE (RED)
= approximately 26 calories per ounce

SPARKLING WINE/CHAMPAGNE
= approximately 30 calories per ounce

PORT/MUSCATEL WINE
= approximately 45 calories per ounce

BEER
= approximately 150 calories in a 12-ounce can or bottle

LIGHT BEER
= approximately 64–110 calories in a 12-ounce bottle

ORANGE JUICE
= approximately 18 calories per ounce

CRANBERRY JUICE
= approximately 15 calories per ounce

GRAPEFRUIT JUICE
= approximately 11 calories per ounce

LEMON AND LIME JUICES
= each approximately 8 calories per ounce

SIMPLE SYRUP
= approximately 18 calories per ounce

▼ HOTTIE Approx 133 calories
(Martini Glass)

Hot peppers not only spice up your love life as natural aphrodisiacs, but also rev up your metabolism! This spicy drink has a double kick from both the tequila and the jalapeños; it's sure to get you ready to shake it on the dance floor.

½ ounce lime juice

1 slice jalapeño

3 drops grapefruit bitters

1 ounce tequila

3 ounces orange juice

2 ounces diet grapefruit soda

1 lime wheel

Muddle lime juice, jalapeño slice, and bitters in the bottom of a mixing glass. Add tequila, orange juice, and ice, then shake. Strain into a martini glass. Top with diet grapefruit soda. Garnish with a lime wheel.

🏆 THE MISSY MULE Approx 78 calories
(Bar Mug)

This is a low-cal version of the classic Moscow Mule, one of the first vodka cocktails; the original was popularized in Hollywood in the mid-20th century. Drinking this version will help you get into film-star shape.

1½ ounces vodka

1 ounce lime juice

4 ounces diet ginger beer (or diet ginger ale)

1 mint sprig

1 lime wheel

Shake vodka and lime juice with ice. Strain into a bar mug (a copper mug is traditional). Fill with ice and top with diet ginger beer. Garnish with a sprig of mint and a lime wheel.

"Buying a pre-owned wedding dress can save you thousands of dollars, and the dress has probably been 'used' for only about five hours (if at all). Do your homework when negotiating the purchase price of a pre-owned gown. Find out the dress's retail price as well as prices of similar pre-owned gowns. And don't be afraid to ask the seller for a discount."

–Josie Daga, founder of PreOwnedWeddingDresses.com

SCHOOLGIRL'S FANTASY Approx 143 calories
(Tall Glass)

This is a grown-up version of an after-school treat—cherry vanilla soda. It may taste like you're cheating on your diet, but you'll get an A+ for calorie control.

1 ounce black cherry vodka

½ ounce Navan vanilla liqueur

4 ounces Hansen's diet black cherry soda

1 maraschino cherry

1 heart-shaped lollipop

Pour vodka and vanilla liqueur into an ice-filled tall glass. Top with diet cherry soda. Stir. Drop a maraschino cherry in the glass and serve it alongside a heart-shaped lollipop.

PERFECT PANACHÉ Approx 35 calories
(Tall Glass)

The Panaché is a refreshing, low-alcohol summertime drink often enjoyed on the Mediterranean coast. This low-cal version is great for a hot afternoon, particularly if you like the taste of beer but want to avoid too many carbs.

> **6 ounces (½ bottle) Miller Genuine Draft 64**
> **3 ounces diet lemon-lime soda**
> **Juice from 1 lemon wedge**
> **1 lemon wheel**

Pour beer and diet soda into an ice-filled tall glass. Squeeze a lemon wedge into the drink. Stir. Garnish with a lemon wheel on the rim of the glass.

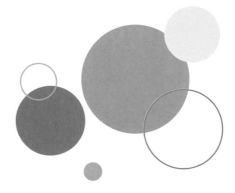

NEGRONITA Approx 120 calories
(Rocks Glass)

This is my low-calorie rendition of the classic Negroni cocktail, originally created in the early 1900s at a bar in Florence in honor of an Italian count by the same name. If you are a nut for the bitter taste of Campari, the herbal notes in a quality gin, and the sweet kiss of red vermouth, this treat will keep you satisfied while you watch your weight.

¾ ounce gin
½ ounce Campari
½ ounce sweet vermouth
Splash diet Fresca
1 orange wheel

Pour gin, Campari, and sweet vermouth into an ice-filled rocks glass. Add a splash of diet Fresca. Stir. Garnish with an orange wheel laid on the surface of the drink.

Econo-tip! I didn't want to force my bridesmaids to shell out a lot of money for an outfit they'd never wear again. So I asked them to buy a dress in my wedding color, in a style that they looked good in and that fit their budget and personality. Funnily enough, everyone wound up with a similar shade of teal, and each attendant looked fantastic. My maid of honor (my sister Amy) has a knack for finding treasures at vintage shops. She scored a simple, elegant dress that fit perfectly and looked very glamorous . . . and cost under $50!

FLY GIRL FROM IPANEMA Approx 78 calories
(Rocks Glass)

Cachaça is a delicious Brazilian rum made from pressed sugarcane. You'll look so good after drinking low-cal cocktails, you'll proudly prance around the beach in your Brazilian-style thong bikini on your honeymoon!

3 mint leaves

½ lime, diced, with peel on

1 ounce cachaça

4 ounces diet Guarana soda (or diet ginger ale)

1 mint sprig

Muddle the mint leaves and lime pieces in the bottom of a rocks glass. Add cachaça and ice and top with diet Guarana soda. Stir. Garnish with a sprig of mint.

▼ SEXY SHEILA Approx 90 calories
(Martini Glass)

Sheila is the Australian equivalent of the American slang *chick* or *Bettie*.
It basically means "girl" and is often used to refer to a cute one. Ozzie's closest neighbors down under are the New Zealanders, otherwise known as Kiwis. Here's a vitamin-packed, low-cal kiwi cocktail for you, you Sexy Sheila!

2 tablespoons diced kiwi

1 ounce mandarin vodka

3 ounces Hansen's diet strawberry kiwi soda

Juice from 1 lime wedge

1 kiwi slice

Muddle diced kiwi in the bottom of a mixing glass. Add vodka, diet soda, juice from lime wedge, and ice and stir. Strain into a chilled martini glass. Garnish with a kiwi slice on the rim of the glass.

4
THE BIG DAY

You've spent the last several months of your life planning, plotting, primping, and preparing to make your wedding day perfect. You've been through dress fittings, bridal showers, cake tastings, gift registry, a million calls to your wedding planner, a million e-mails with your maid of honor, and a million little decisions with your fiancé. So let's finally delve into the whole reason you bought this book: the wedding itself!

Cocktail recipes from any section of this book will work beautifully for your actual wedding. If you found something you love among the champagne cocktails, or the suggestions for the engagement party, or even the great drinks shared by some of my "drinking buddies" for the bachelor party, know that any of those drinks are totally appropriate for the nuptial dinner and reception.

In this chapter I present some more liquid inspiration to round out your arsenal of cocktail recipes, which I hope are already serving you well and will continue to do so long into your marriage. Below you'll find some ideas for themed weddings and destination weddings and, finally, a few tips for you, the bubbly bride on your big day.

PREPARING FOR THE BIG WALK

If you're having an afternoon wedding, it may be tempting to quell your nerves with a glass of champagne. If you decide to indulge (I had one while my hair was being done), make sure you don't overdo it. And, most importantly, make sure you eat breakfast! There is no more surefire way to make yourself dizzy and become easily inebriated than starting out on an empty stomach.

KIR ROYALE
(Champagne Flute)

This easy-to-make, tasty classic champagne cocktail would be lovely to sip with your bridal party while getting ready, or with your father in a special toast before he walks his little girl down the aisle.

> **1 ounce crème de cassis**
> **4 ounces sparkling wine**
> **1 lemon twist (optional)**

Pour ingredients into a wine glass. Garnish with a lemon twist, if desired.

It is a nice gesture to offer guests refreshment as they arrive at your wedding. Depending on the venue, alcohol may not be appropriate; lemonade and iced mint tea are simple yet universally pleasing options.

GOING GREEN AT YOUR WHITE WEDDING

Being eco-friendly is more than a trend; it's a way of life. There is more interest than ever in bringing some "green" touches to a white wedding. Whether you print invitations on recycled paper in soy ink, choose an organic caterer, or even buy a vintage wedding dress, there are many ways to bring environmental consciousness into your special day. One of the most fun ways, of course, is at the bar!

I started offering The Liquid Muse Sustainable Sips cocktail classes in Los Angeles in 2006, and by the end of 2008 I had taught nearly 1,000 people around the United States how to mix and shake eco-friendly drinks. Keep your eyes open for certified organic, environmentally friendly, and otherwise sustainable spirits and wines. There are a slew of them coming onto the market, and I am excited every time I learn of a new one.

"Being 'eco-chic' doesn't mean you need to have a 'green-themed' wedding. It just means you make responsible choices while still planning the wedding of your dreams."

–Sarah Hubbell, owner of The Wedding Hub, Phoenix, AZ

DETOX AMERICA COCKTAIL
(Martini Glass)

Method Home nontoxic cleaning products partnered with The Liquid Muse Sustainable Sips (my eco-cocktail program) for their "Detox America" campaign. As a featured educator in their nationwide program, I taught "greenies" around the country how to make a sustainable lifestyle more fun! The tart flavor and antioxidant qualities of the açai berry paired with healthful pomegranate juice and ginger in this drink is a refreshing way to get both vitamins and an eco-friendly party in one glass!

½ ounce VeeV açai spirit

1½ ounces organic vodka or gin

2 ounces organic pomegranate juice

½ ounce lime juice

¾ ounce agave nectar

Pinch freshly grated ginger

Pour all ingredients except ginger into a cocktail shaker. Add ice and shake well. Strain into a martini glass. Grate fresh ginger over the top of the cocktail.

☙ HOT ROD CADILLAC

(Martini Glass)

It took me until I was in my 30s to develop a proper appreciation for tequila. I'd had tequila shots in college and felt horrible afterward. Now that I've had a chance to learn about the spirit and appreciate its rich flavor, history, and incredible versatility, I love experimenting with it! This is my signature margarita made with my favorite organic tequila.

Course sea salt

1 slice jalapeño

¾ ounce lime juice

¾ ounce agave nectar

1½ ounces freshly squeezed organic grapefruit juice

2 ounces 4 Copas organic tequila

½ ounce orange liqueur (optional)

Rim one-third of a martini glass with course sea salt. Set aside. Muddle jalapeño and lime juice in the bottom of a mixing glass. Add agave nectar, grapefruit juice, tequila, and orange liqueur. Shake well and gently strain into the glass.

"Bridal couples looking to 'green' their weddings might consider eco-friendly invitations. Several organizations offer recycled paper invitations and can even embed them with seeds so you can grow wildflowers with the invites after the wedding is over!"

–Nancy Phillips, general manager of handmade stationery store WomanCraft, Chicago, IL

▼ THE LIQUID MUSE "GREEN" AND WHITE SANGRIA

(Makes 16 servings; Wine Goblet)

I love serving sangria because it is easy to prepare and the taste of fresh fruits makes it a real crowd-pleaser. I enjoy wandering the local farmer's market to see which fruits are seasonal whenever I'm going to make it. Using white wine is a pleasant variation and allows the colorful fruit to be seen.

2 cups diced seasonal organic fruits, skins on*

½ cup organic nectar (summer: peach; fall: pear)

½ cup VeeV açai spirit

2 bottles Bonterra wine (summer: sauvignon blanc; fall: chardonnay)

Marinate the diced fruit in organic nectar and VeeV for at least 2 hours. Fifteen minutes before guests are due to arrive, ladle two heaping tablespoons of fruit into each wine goblet, making sure to get a little of the juice mixture, too. As guests arrive, fill each glass with ice and top with wine.

*SUMMER: strawberries, peaches, cherries, kiwi
  FALL: apples, pears, figs, grapes, kumquats

NUTS ABOUT YOU
(Champagne Flute)

The dark fruits and almond in this sparkling cocktail pair nicely with an elegant evening reception. Since developing this recipe a few years ago, I have made it a staple in my house over the holidays.

1 lime slice

2 teaspoons organic sugar

2–3 drops organic almond extract

1 sour cherry

¾ ounce Casal dos Jordoes tawny port (organically grown grapes)

3½ ounces Can Vendrell Cava Brut Reserva (organically grown grapes)

Sugar-rim a champagne flute by rubbing the rim with a lime, then dipping it into sugar. Pour 1 teaspoon of sugar into bottom of flute, then add almond extract. Drop in sour cherry. Gently pour in port, then top with cava.

Pairing food with cocktails rather than wine is a hot new trend. If you decide to jump on the bandwagon, do not pair your meal courses with sweet, dessert-style drinks. Opt instead for cocktails made with muddled herbs and lighter flavors.

GARDEN WEDDING

Standing under the leafy boughs of century-old trees with fragrant blooming flowers overhead gave my outdoor wedding an ethereal quality. Choosing a natural backdrop can be a magical setting for exchanging vows as well as posing for wedding photos.

♥ BLUEBERRY LAVENDER LEMONADE
(Wine Glass)

This lemonade punch is fragrant, slightly sweet, and colorful enough for a special celebration. If you're being married in a warm destination or on a hot summer day, this will keep your guests cool and satisfied.

1 ounce blueberry vodka

½ ounce lemoncello

¾ ounce Sonoma lavender syrup

¾ ounce lemon juice

2 ounces prosecco

1 lemon wheel

Shake vodka, lemoncello, lavender syrup, and lemon juice with ice. Strain into a white wine glass. Add prosecco and stir. Place lemon wheel on the rim of the glass for garnish.

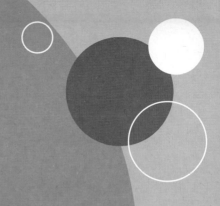

🍷 LOVE IN BLOOM
(Wine Glass)

I designed this cocktail for my friends Jackie and Tony in honor of their
garden wedding at a breathtaking, historic estate in Georgetown, a swanky
neighborhood in Washington DC. As they finished exchanging their vows
and the reception began, guests were presented with this refreshing and
romantic drink.

> **1 heaping tablespoon diced cucumber, seeded and peeled**
> **1 ounce rose-infused simple syrup, page 9**
> **½ ounce freshly squeezed lemon juice**
> **2 ounces Hendrick's gin**
> **Splash soda water**
> **1 edible flower**

Muddle cucumber, simple syrup, and lemon juice in the bottom
of a mixing glass. Add ice and gin and shake vigorously. Strain
into a chilled wine glass. Top with a splash of soda water. Garnish with an edible flower floating on the surface of the drink.
(This can also be served in a tall glass filled with ice.)

GARDEN MOJITO
(Tall Glass)

Cucumber has been popping up in cocktails for the last few years, with good reason! The clean taste of garden-fresh vegetables invokes a relaxing day at the spa.

1 heaping tablespoon diced organic cucumber

1 heaping tablespoon diced organic lime

1 heaping teaspoon raw brown sugar

6–7 torn mint leaves

1½ ounces organic vodka

Splash organic Italian lemon spritzer (or lemon-flavored soda water)

1 mint sprig or lime wheel

Muddle cucumber, lime, sugar, and mint leaves in a tall glass. Pour in vodka. Top with spritzer. Garnish with a sprig of mint or lime wheel.

ASIAN FLAIR

The elegant beauty of Asian culture lends itself to a special event such as a wedding. Consider incorporating Asian flowers, food, and drinks into your reception for extra style.

The following cocktail recipes make use of the spirits sake and shochu (or soju). Sake is a fermented rice beverage often called "rice wine." It has a light flavor and is a delightful change of pace on its own and in cocktails. Hot sake is widely consumed in the United States, but most of the higher-quality sakes are served chilled. Shochu is a clear spirit distilled from grains, rice, or even sweet potato. It is sometimes used in place of vodka—one benefit being that it is lower in both alcohol content and calories.

"Couples wanting an exotic Asian theme could include a vintage Japanese wedding kimono in the big event. These dazzling art pieces are decorated with fans, cranes, or festive florals. Imagine the elegant brocade draped over the bride's shoulders and then displayed behind the head table during the reception!"

–Nancy McDonough, owner of Kyoto Kimono, Endicott, NY

♥ SWEET PEA COCKTAIL
(Cocktail Glass)

When developing this cocktail, I loved the idea of infusing delicate snap peas with subtly aromatic shochu. I aimed to create a drink that could stand on its own but still lend itself to sushi pairings without being too sweet or overpowering.

2 ounces sugar snap pea–infused shochu*
¾ ounce brewed and cooled jasmine tea
¼ ounce simple syrup, page 9
1 sugar snap pea on a bamboo skewer

Shake infused shochu, tea, and simple syrup with ice. Strain into small cocktail glass or martini glass. Garnish with a snap pea on a bamboo skewer across the rim of the glass.

*SUGAR SNAP PEA–INFUSED SHOCHU: Add 4–5 sugar peas (or snap peas) to a 750-milliliter bottle of shochu and let stand for at least 24 hours.

▼ THE RISING SUN SAKE MARTINI
(Martini Glass)

David Roth, who created this saketini, can be found behind the bar in Hartford, Connecticut. His knowledge stretches all the way to Japan, where he honed his sake skills alongside the experts. The earthy sweetness of plum wine plays nicely with the subtle sake, and when the grenadine sinks to the bottom of the glass, it makes a lovely layered effect.

1 ounce chilled sake

1 ounce plum wine

½ ounce orange juice

½ ounce pineapple juice

¼ ounce grenadine

1 cherry

Shake sake, plum wine, and juices with ice. Strain into a chilled martini glass. Slowly add the grenadine so that it will sink to the bottom, creating a layered effect. Garnish with a cherry on a wooden skewer placed across the rim of the glass.

ASIAN MARTINI

(Martini Glass)

Drawing from popular Asian ingredients, this cocktail softly highlights exotic flair. I love muddled lychees in all kinds of cocktails, and ginger is a no-brainer in Far East food and drink.

2 lychees
1¼-inch-thick slice fresh ginger
1½ ounces shochu or soju
¾ ounce dry sake
Dash orange water

Muddle 1 lychee and ginger slice in the bottom of a mixing glass. Add all liquid ingredients, shake with ice, and strain into chilled martini glass. Drop the other lychee into the bottom of the cocktail.

Get Exotic

Hindu brides adorn themselves with ornate gold jewelry, exotic jewels affixed to their foreheads, and mendhi hand painting for the bridal party before the big day. During the wedding the couple exchanges flower garlands, takes seven steps around a fire, and incorporates red into the ceremony, a traditional color symbolizing joy.

TROPICAL ENCOUNTERS

Sometimes the destination defines the theme of a wedding, and many couples decide to tie the knot in the same area where they'd like to honeymoon. Whether in Hawaii, the Caribbean, or any other exotic location, an island beachfront is one of the most beautiful and fun places for you and your guests. Exotic juices and different kinds of rum make for fabulous cocktails in the tropics.

"As a Destination Wedding bride, your relationship with your wedding planner is very important since she is the one 'on the ground' acting on your behalf. Find out the company's refund policy on cancellations and what backup plans are in place for bad weather. Be clear about what you want from your planner; her aim is for you to be pleased. Then on the big day you can relax and enjoy!"

–Joy Basdeo, owner and manager of
Simply Weddings, Grand Cayman

▼ THE CLASSIC PIÑA COLADA
(Tall Glass or Large Cocktail Glass)

This version of the beachside favorite was created in 1957 in Puerto Rico, using the new coconut cream known as Coco Lopez. The drink is creamy, fruity, and decadent, and when made according to this recipe, it is the quintessential tropical treat.

- **1½ ounces light rum**
- **1 ounce Meyers dark rum**
- **2 ounces Coco Lopez**
- **1 ounce cream**
- **4 ounces fresh pineapple juice**
- **1 cup crushed ice**
- **2 pineapple wedges**
- **1 cherry**

Blend rums, Coco Lopez, cream, pineapple juice, crushed ice, and 1 pineapple wedge in an electric blender for 15 seconds. Pour into a tall glass or fancy large cocktail glass. Garnish with the other pineapple wedge and a cherry.

Drink with a Plan
Don't start your first day as a "Mrs." with a pounding head! Avoid a hangover with these tips:
- Water, water, water—follow each alcoholic drink with a glass of water
- Don't forget to eat
- Go easy on sugary drinks
- Take an aspirin before bed

❦ FANTASY ISLAND MIMOSA
(Champagne Flute)

This is my variation on the perfect breakfast or lunchtime champagne cocktail. Why stick with orange juice when you are in the tropics? Go for the luscious juices the islands have to offer, and even get playful by rimming the glass with crackling candy!

1 lemon wedge

1 package Pop Rocks candy

¾ ounce pineapple juice

¾ ounce guava juice

2 ounces champagne

½ ounce grenadine

Rub the rim of a champagne flute with a lemon wedge. Pour about 2 tablespoons of Pop Rocks onto a small, dry plate. Dip glass rim into the crackling candy so that the pieces stick to it. Pour juices and champagne into the flute. Slowly add the grenadine, allowing it to sink to the bottom. Try to make and serve the drink quickly so the candy still crackles when someone brings the glass to their lips.

The Juice Bar
Set up a special juice bar at the wedding where kids and adults alike can get colorful, liquor-free mocktails in fancy glasses. Even those who don't drink alcohol can still be in on the fun! (Want more virgin mixology ideas? Pick up a copy of *Preggatinis: Mixology for the Mom-to-Be*.)

GINGER PASSION FIZZ

(Tall Glass or Tiki Mug)

Tiki cocktail enthusiast Matt Robold of RumDood.com created this cocktail. He notes that it can be made as a single serving or scaled up to make a tiki punch. This kind of drink is sweet enough for grandma but strong enough for dear old dad.

½ ounce lime juice

1 ounce passion fruit liqueur

1½ ounces gold rum

¼ ounce amaretto

¼ ounce simple syrup (optional), page 9

¾ ounce ginger beer (or ginger ale)

¼ ounce dark rum

Pour lime juice through simple syrup into a mixing glass. Shake with ice, then strain into an ice-filled tall glass or tiki mug. Top with ginger beer. Give one good stir. Slowly pour in the dark rum to "float" on the surface of the drink.

TROPICAL TEASER
(Wine Glass)

I believe that cocktails are supposed to be fun and creative, so I experiment with spirits *and* wine when creating new drinks. You may not expect mango and mint in your pinot grigio, but why not give it a try?

- **1 heaping tablespoon diced fresh mango**
- **3 torn mint leaves**
- **1 teaspoon sugar**
- **¼ ounce lime juice**
- **2 ounces pinot grigio (or other light white wine)**
- **1 lime wheel**

Muddle mango, mint, sugar, and lime juice in the bottom of a mixing glass or cocktail shaker. Fill with ice and add wine. Shake vigorously and strain into a chilled wine glass. Place the lime wheel on the rim of the glass.

DESSERT DRINKS

Cake isn't the only sweets option for your reception. Why not simply present your guests with a plate of fancy cookies and a tray of pint-size dessert cocktails? Colorful, sweet, creamy, and decadent, dessert cocktails can be a delightful replacement for (or accompaniment to) the traditional last course.

These first two drinks, the Grasshopper and the Pink Squirrel, came out of the post–World War II cocktail boom in the United States.

GRASSHOPPER
(Cocktail Glass)

Do you love a chocolate mint after dinner? This creamy little cocktail could easily become a favorite substitute!

¾ ounce white chocolate liqueur
¾ ounce crème de menthe, green
¾ ounce cream

Shake all ingredients with ice. Strain into a chilled cocktail glass.

PINK SQUIRREL
(Cocktail Glass)

This chocolaty, creamy cocktail with hazelnut liqueur would tempt any cocktail-loving critter.

¾ ounce white chocolate liqueur
¾ ounce crème de noyaux
¾ ounce cream

Shake all ingredients with ice. Strain into a chilled cocktail glass.

▼ CHOCOLATE RASPBERRY MINTINI
(Martini Glass)

Who doesn't love chocolate? This drink is a dessert unto itself, and it is delicious! I strongly suggest not serving a chocolate dessert with a chocolate cocktail. (There can be a sensory overload of a good thing!) It would, however, be lovely with a lemon tart or a small plate of meringue cookies.

Red decorating sugar

6 fresh raspberries

3–4 leaves fresh mint

1½ ounces raspberry vodka

1 ounce Godiva chocolate liqueur

½ ounce Chambord

½ ounce cream

Rim a martini glass with red decorating sugar and set aside. Muddle 3 raspberries and the mint leaves in the bottom of a cocktail shaker. Add raspberry vodka, chocolate liqueur, Chambord, and cream. Shake with ice. Gently strain into martini glass. Garnish with the remaining 3 raspberries on a cocktail pick on the rim of the glass.

▼ ORANGE CREAMSICLE
(Cocktail Glass)

This vanilla-orange sensation would be lovely alongside a rich chocolate torte or even carrot cake.

1½ ounces orange vodka
¾ ounce Cointreau
¾ ounce Navan vanilla liqueur
½ ounce cream

Shake all ingredients with ice. Strain into a cocktail glass.

▼ LEMON CHIFFON PIE
(Martini Glass)

If any dessert flavor rivals chocolate in popularity, it's lemon! The same goes for dessert drinks. This silky cocktail pairs easily with everything from chocolate cake to seasonal berries with a dollop of whipped cream.

Cocktail Candy Lemon Twist rimmer

1½ ounces lemon-flavored vodka

¾ ounce lemoncello

½ ounce Navan vanilla liqueur

½ ounce lime juice

1 small egg white

Dash lemon bitters (optional)

Rim a martini glass with Lemon Twist rimmer. Set aside. Shake all other ingredients vigorously with ice. Gently strain into the rimmed glass.

▼ CHERRY APPLE COBBLER
(Martini Glass)

Created by Pablo Moix, a head mixologist at the celebrity-studded, see-and-be-seen STK restaurants in Los Angeles and New York, this dessert drink would be especially wonderful for a harvest-themed wedding because apples are in season and freshly pressed cider is readily available at the local farmer's market.

1 graham cracker, finely ground
1 bar spoon cherry preserves
1 ounce apple eau de vie
1 ounce rum
½ ounce simple syrup, page 9
½ ounce heavy cream
1 ounce apple cider
1 dollop whipped cream

Rim a martini glass with finely ground graham cracker dust. Set aside. Shake preserves and all liquid ingredients in a cocktail shaker. Gently strain into a martini glass. Top with whipped cream.

♼ GINGERBREAD SIDECAR
(Martini Glass)

This recipe comes from Kylee Van Dillen, a Los Angeles–based bartender who has a penchant for creating cookie cocktails. The gingerbread spices make it ideal for a winter wedding.

Fine sugar

Pinch each ground ginger, ground cloves, and ground cinnamon

2 ounces cognac

¾ ounce fresh lemon juice

½ ounce freshly squeezed orange juice

½ ounce gingerbread syrup

¼ ounce Cointreau

2 dashes Angostura bitters

1 orange twist

Rim a martini glass with a mixture of superfine sugar blended with pinches of the ground spices. Set aside. Shake all liquid ingredients and bitters with ice and gently strain into the rimmed glass. Garnish with an orange twist.

5
HAPPILY EVER AFTER

Now relax. Close your eyes. Take a deep breath in, and let it out slowly. Gently, open your eyes and look around your new life. You did it! You are a married lady. You and your husband are about to embark on the journey that follows wedding planning—sacred matrimony. For better or worse, in sickness and in health, rolling in money or drowning in debt, this is the guy who will be by your side. From now on he is your life partner and most cherished friend.

Every celebration since the proposal has involved a group of people. Friends and family have a stake in this union, and they wanted to be part of it. However, once the rings are exchanged, the cake is cut, and the bouquet is tossed, you and your groom finally get to be alone . . . at least for the wedding night. (Sometimes, the wedding itself is so hectic that you barely have a chance to spend quality time with your groom while playing hostess at the reception.) Arrange for a special bottle of champagne to be on ice wherever you are spending the wedding night so the two of you can enjoy a private toast. Most of all, make an effort to do that from time to time throughout your marriage. Showing appreciation for one another will keep your bond strong and have you feeling as in love ten years from now as you do today.

STEP INTO MY BOUDOIR

Why not create a very special present to give your groom on the wedding night or first wedding anniversary? Hire a professional photographer to photograph you in lingerie and put the pictures into a small album, for his eyes only. You can theme the photos to reflect his fantasies—the sassy cheerleader or naughty librarian, a vintage pinup or leather-clad dominatrix, or perhaps a sultry 1950s housewife mixing her man a martini. Get creative and have fun! Enlisting one of your girlfriends to assist during the shoot will help you be less nervous—and provide someone to laugh with along the way.

❙ THE TROUSSEAU TICKLER
(Champagne Flute)

This cocktail is kissed with flowery elegance. It makes for a wonderful "greeting" cocktail at bridal showers and wedding receptions. It is also a beautiful drink for you and your groom once the reception is over.

> **3½ ounces chilled champagne**
> **Dash rhubarb bitters (optional)**
> **½ ounce St. Germain elderflower liqueur**
> **¼ ounce Chambord**
> **1 hibiscus flower in syrup**

Pour champagne into flute first, followed by the bitters. Then, slowly add the elderflower liqueur. Its viscosity will make it settle at the bottom of the glass. Next, very gently add the Chambord. It will settle just above the elderflower liqueur, creating a slightly layered effect. Finally, drop in the hibiscus flower.

VERY SEXY COCKTAIL
(Cocktail Glass)

Tony Abou Ganim, also known as The Modern Mixologist, develops bar programs for hotel chains, cruise lines, and liquor companies. Tony's great "barside manner" has won him many female admirers, and this drink of his is like a whirlwind romance: sweet, tart, and bubbly!

1½ ounces Belvedere Cytrus vodka

½ ounce Marie Brizard Cassis de Bordeaux

1½ ounces fresh lemon sour*

Marinated wild berries

1 ounce chilled Moet White Star champagne

In an ice-filled shaker add Belvedere, cassis, and fresh sour; shake until well blended. Strain into a chilled cocktail glass with marinated berries in the bottom. Top with champagne.

*****LEMON SOUR:** Combine equal parts simple syrup and freshly squeezed lemon juice.

In addition to booking a sexy boudoir photo shoot, some brides also give their wedding gown one final fling. Claire Barrett, who shot the cocktails for this book and my previous book, *Preggatinis,* is also a sought-after wedding photographer. She says, "Lots of brides are getting more mileage from their couture dress by scheduling a fantasy fashion shoot after the wedding day, when *demure* can be left at the altar!"

DAY-AFTER DRINKS

Unless you are rushing off to your honeymoon destination the next morning, it is a nice gesture to arrange a casual day-after brunch. Assuming your guests have had a great party the night before, they could be in the mood for a late-morning meal and perhaps a little "hair of the dog." Keep it light. Brunch cocktails should be refreshing (and sometimes served with a side of aspirin!).

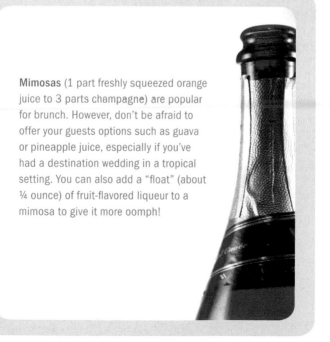

Mimosas (1 part freshly squeezed orange juice to 3 parts champagne) are popular for brunch. However, don't be afraid to offer your guests options such as guava or pineapple juice, especially if you've had a destination wedding in a tropical setting. You can also add a "float" (about ¼ ounce) of fruit-flavored liqueur to a mimosa to give it more oomph!

THE ULTIMATE BLOODY MARY BAR

The Bloody Mary is the go-to morning-after drink for most people. The standard for this drink is about 1 part vodka to 4 parts tomato juice. However, it can also be made with tequila (called a Bloody Maria) or gin (called a Red Snapper) for an equally delicious morning cocktail.

One of the fun things about a Bloody Mary is the myriad of ways it can be garnished and flavored. From bacon to wasabi, people take the personalization of their drinks seriously! Setting up a self-serve "drink buffet" is a fun way to provide options for just about every taste. On the next page, I've suggested essential ingredients and garnishes to make your Bloody Mary Bar the most extensive your guests have ever seen!

Tomato juice	Chili peppers	Lemongrass
Tomato water*	Cilantro	Olives
Bacon	Cocktail onions	Pickles
Basil	Ginger	Rosemary
Beef consommé	Green beans	Soy sauce
Cracked black pepper	Horseradish	Tabasco
Celery	Miso	Wasabi
Celery salt	Lemon	Worcestershire sauce

*TOMATO WATER: Freeze 6–8 large tomatoes in a glass bowl overnight. Take the bowl out the next morning and allow the tomatoes to thaw in it. Collect the liquid at the bottom of the bowl in a small pitcher. Next, gently pull the peel off each tomato and discard. Take each tomato between your hands and hold it over the pitcher. Press firmly, letting the juice fall into the pitcher. (Save the tomato "meat" in a small bowl to use for a tomato sauce.) Pour the liquid in the pitcher through a small strainer into a jar. The liquid will be pinkish but clear. This tomato water is a nice variation from thicker tomato juice. Save unused tomato water in the refrigerator for up to 3 days.

History of the Bloody Mary
The Bloody Mary was first created by Ferdinand Petiot at Harry's New York Bar in Paris in the 1920s when post WWI tomato juice cans found their way into the bar and were mixed with "a clear neutral spirit." Petiot later brought the drink back to the United States when he returned after Prohibition. Voilà, the birth of an enduring classic drink!

MEXICAN MICHELADA

(Tall Glass)

Some guests might want to try a unique and thirst-quenching beer cocktail. This one adds South of the Border flair to a brunch or backyard barbeque. (Later, it can also bring a change of pace to taco night at home with the hubby.)

3 ounces tomato juice

¼ ounce lemon juice

¼ ounce lime juice

Dash Tabasco

Dash Worcestershire sauce

4 ounces pale Mexican beer

1 leafy sprig cilantro

Pour juices and condiments into a chilled tall glass. Add beer and stir. Garnish with cilantro sprig.

There is no better way to say thank you than by throwing a party. Why not organize one final soiree—even something as simple as serving pizza and your signature cocktail—for that inner circle of people who worked so hard to make your wedding perfect? You'll get to use your new home bar with the added bonus of forcing everyone to ooh and aah over your wedding album, too!

LA VIE EN ROSE
(Champagne Flute)

La vie en rose literally translates to "Life in pink." It is the equivalent of the English saying "Life through rose-colored glasses." Finding a soul mate can make anyone see the world through a rosy hue. This drink was created by Eric Alperin, who also created The Ruse in the Boys' Night Out section of this book.

½ ounce lime juice
¾ ounce rosemary-honey syrup*
2–3 drops rosewater
1 ounce cachaça
Rose champagne
1 rose blossom

Combine lime juice, rosemary-honey syrup, rosewater, and cachaça in a shaking tin. Add ice and do a light toss. Strain into a champagne flute and top with rose champagne. Garnish with a rose blossom of any color.

*ROSEMARY-HONEY SYRUP: Mix ½ cup honey and 1 cup hot water in a bar tumbler. Steep ½ cup fresh rosemary in liquid until cool. Strain out rosemary and store syrup in the refrigerator. Makes 1 to 1½ cups.

Index

About the Author

Beverage consultant and mixologist
Natalie Bovis-Nelsen is the editor of
TheLiquidMuse.com, which bridges
the gap between the spirits industry
and the everyday consumer.

In addition to writing about
cocktails, she provides brand
consultation to alcoholic and
nonalcoholic beverage companies
and teaches cocktail classes around
the country. She has appeared on
regional and national television
and radio shows, and hosts video
podcasts (found on her website) highlighting cocktail culture.
Natalie is also the author of *Preggatinis: Mixology for the Mom-to-Be,* which launched to rave reviews and was included in
about.com's Best Cocktail Books of 2008.

Whether you're reaching for *The Bubbly Bride* or
Preggatinis, Natalie hopes to inspire you to incorporate quality
mixology into your home entertaining. Visit www.theliquidmuse
.com for more cocktailian tidbits and to join The Liquid Muse
Cocktail Club.

With an eye toward not only what goes into the glass
but how it's presented, Natalie served as drink stylist for the
photos featured throughout this book.